SACRED CONVERSATIONS AND THE EVOLUTION OF DIALOGUE

MARIANNE FARINA, CSC

2016 Madeleva Lecture in Spirituality

Paulist Press
New York / Mahwah, NJ

Permission to reprint "The Bee and the Pulley" and "*Serenitas*" courtesy of Eva Mary Hooker, CSC.

Cover and book design by Lynn Else

Library of Congress Cataloging-in-Publication Data
Names: Farina, Marianne, author.
Title: Sacred conversations and the evolution of dialogue / Marianne Farina, CSC.
Description: New York : Paulist Press, 2017. | Series: 2016 Madeleva lecture in spirituality
Identifiers: LCCN 2017000275 (print) | LCCN 2017023946 (ebook) | ISBN 9781587686351 (ebook) | ISBN 9780809153015 (pbk. : alk. paper)
Subjects: LCSH: Spirituality—Catholic Church. | Catholic Church—Relations—Islam. | Islam—Relations—Catholic Church. | Sisters of the Holy Cross.
Classification: LCC BX2350.65 (ebook) | LCC BX2350.65 .F37 2017 (print) | DDC 255/.97—dc23
LC record available at https://lccn.loc.gov/2017000275

ISBN 978-0-8091-5301-5 (paperback)
ISBN 978-1-58768-635-1 (e-book)

Published by Paulist Press
997 Macarthur Boulevard
Mahwah, New Jersey 07430

www.paulistpress.com

Printed and bound in the
United States of America

SACRED CONVERSATIONS AND THE EVOLUTION OF DIALOGUE **Sacred Conversations and the Evolution of Dialogue** Sacred Conversations and the Evolution of Dialogue SACRED CONVERSATIONS AND THE EVOLUTION OF DIALOGUE **Sacred Conversations and the Evolution of Dialogue** Sacred Conversations and the Evolution of Dialogue SACRED CONVERSATIONS AND THE EVOLUTION OF DIALOGUE **Sacred Conversations and the Evolution of Dialogue** Sacred Conversations and the Evolution of Dialogue SACRED CONVERSATIONS AND THE EVOLUTION OF DIALOGUE **Sacred Conversations and the Evolution of Dialogue** Sacred Conversations and the Evolution of Dialogue SACRED CONVERSATIONS AND THE EVOLUTION OF DIALOGUE **Sacred Conversations and the Evolution of Dialogue** Sacred Conversations and the Evolution of Dialogue SACRED CONVERSATIONS AND THE EVOLUTION OF DIALOGUE **Sacred Conversations and the Evolution of Dialogue** Sacred Conversations and the Evolution of Dialogue SACRED CONVERSATIONS AND THE EVOLUTION OF DIALOGUE **Sacred Conversations and the Evolution of Dialogue** Sacred Conversations and the Evolution of Dialogue SACRED CONVERSATIONS AND THE EVOLUTION OF DIALOGUE

CONTENTS

PREFACE

Named in honor of Sr. Madeleva Wolff, CSC, who founded a School of Sacred Theology for women (1944–69) at Saint Mary's College, the Center for Spirituality's Madeleva Lecture Series has provided an important platform for women's contributions to Christian theology and spirituality for over thirty years. These lectures have focused on the multifaceted nature of spirituality, the fruit of spirituality in its works for justice and peace, and the growth of a global spirituality capable of addressing needs and concerns in church and society. Publishing the lecture series has enabled these important studies to reach a larger audience across national and international campuses and faith communities. As such the lecture series remains firm in its pledge to young women articulated in the 2000 *Madeleva Manifesto* to continue energetic dialogue about issues of freedom and responsibility for women as all traditions join in imagining the great *shalom* of God.

My lecture sought to capture both this historical foundation and the dynamic of the series. First, the lecture commemorates the 175th anniversary of the foundation of the Sisters of the Holy Cross, founders and sponsors of Saint Mary's College, by inviting a Sister of the Holy Cross to present this year's Madeleva lecture. Second, the theme for the lecture emerges from the apostolic vision of the congregation, which in many ways represents the dynamic of energetic dialogue. Engaging in interreligious, intercultural, and interdisciplinary conversations throughout the world, the Sisters of the Holy Cross remain steadfast to their call to be women of compassion, bearing witness to God's desire for the transformation of human hearts and human relationships.

Moreover, in keeping with Sr. Madeleva's inspiration, as well as this year's theme, the lecture was accompanied by poetry composed by Eva Mary Hooker, CSC, for the occasion. It also included a response by Asma Afsaruddin, an Islamic scholar who has contributed to critical dialogues and comparative studies around the world. Thus the evening represented not only in content but also in form the spirit of the Madeleva Lecture Series.

Additionally, this year's program can serve as a model for interreligious dialogue. The lecture and its accompanying pieces served as the focus for the New Voices seminar the following day. In those discussions, the topic of dialogue and spirituality was explored by women theologians, historians, and anthropologists along with women students taking courses in religious studies at Saint Mary's College. What emerged in these endeavors was a recommitment to explore across campuses and in society ways for women to engage in prophetic dialogues, bringing into our theological and social imaginaries the great *shalom* of God.

Marianne Farina, CSC

INTRODUCTION

History illustrates how religions and cultures meeting in a number of ways and in varying global contexts have had a formative impact on faith traditions. The positive and negative effects of these encounters are readily identifiable in sacred texts, philosophical and theological teachings, and social histories. In recent years, especially after September 11, 2001, projects devoted to promoting Christian-Muslim relations, that is, building bridges between faith communities, highlighted the importance of acknowledging this enduring fact. These partnerships focus on promoting the common good and the study of Christian and Islamic teachings.[1] Some have included workshops that train leaders for dialogue.[2]

The programs have created the critical groundwork for dialogue and also indicate ways to enhance and expand Christian-Muslim dialogue.[3] Such developments are urgently needed today because, despite the good work accomplished thus far, Islamophobia and violent clashes between Muslims and Christians are on the rise. We see evidence of this phenomenon in the United States as a recent study reports that only 14 percent of Catholics in the United States have positive views of Islam.[4] Dialogues capable of reversing these discouraging trends will help believers realize that difference is not a threat to undermining their beliefs. In fact, remaining rooted in one's own spiritual heritage facilitates the authentic sharing of traditions. This learning across traditions deepens faith; the dialogues are a means for deepening that faith and growing in love for God and others. In this essay, I propose that sacred conversations are a type of wellspring for this spirituality of dialogue.

Sacred conversations are interreligious encounters dedicated to the interior movements of the spirit in dialogue and study. Sacred conversations nurture faith because as we pass over from our truth to another's and back to our own,[5] we enrich our grasp of truth and faith commitments. This growth helps us cultivate a deep theological ethic, an ethic similar to the movements of deep ecological systems signaling evolutionary change through innovation and cooperation; they foster a greater sense of belonging and solidarity between religions and cultures.

In what follows, I will continue to describe the meaning of sacred conversation and the evolution of dialogue. Part 1 is a reflection on two significant anniversaries that gives shape to my proposal, identifying the context for my description of the sacred conversations. Part 2 explains in detail my proposal for dialogues as sacred conversations and shows how resources from Catholic and Islamic teachings and studies in dialogue and comparative theology support this approach. Part 3 offers three examples of interreligious engagements in which sacred conversations are either already unfolding or will yet provide a major contribution to the growth of these programs. The first example describes the current state of the Congregation of Holy Cross's collaboration with Islam in Bangladesh. The second profiles academic centers and seminaries that have incorporated inter-religious approaches to theological learning. The third example highlights social organizations creating innovative forums for the meeting of religions and cultures. I conclude the book with some recommendations based on these examples and the overall proposal.

PART I

OUR COMMUNITIES, OUR CONVERSATIONS

The context for my proposal that interreligious learning deepens through practices of sacred conversations emerges from reflections connected to two anniversaries: first, the fiftieth anniversary of *Nostra aetate* (1965) promulgated at the Second Vatican Council, along with the closing of this Council; second, the 175th anniversary of the founding of the Congregation of the Sisters of the Holy Cross.

SECOND VATICAN COUNCIL (1962–1965)

Programs of dialogue and lecture series commemorating the fiftieth anniversary of the closing of the Second Vatican Council offered opportunities to reflect on the Spirit's movement in the Church through the Council's deliberations, especially regarding the Church's commitment to promote ecumenical and interreligious relations. Four out of the Council's sixteen documents address the Church's interreligious relations. The dogmatic constitution of the Council, *Lumen gentium* (LG), speaks of the people of God as those who proclaim God as Creator (no. 16), and all of goodwill as partners with the Church in fulfilling God's plan of salvation. For, as the document states, beyond the visible boundaries of the Church, many elements of truth and holiness can be found (LG 8). *Ad gentes* (AG), a document focusing on renewal of the Church's missionary activity, states that dialogue can reveal the "treasures a generous God has distributed among the nations of the earth" (no. 11).

Gaudium et spes (GS), the Second Vatican Council's apostolic constitution, highlights dialogue in the articulation of the Church's call to read the signs of the times (no. 4). Thus the Church seeks to be a compassionate presence for all people: "The joys and the hopes, the griefs and the anxieties of the men [*sic*] of this age, especially those who are poor or in any way afflicted, these are the joys and hopes, the griefs and anxieties of the followers of Christ. Indeed, nothing genuinely human fails to raise an echo in their hearts" (GS 1). Three essential beliefs animate this mission: (1) all humans are made in God's image and therefore possess dignity; (2) the Church is called to serve humanity in all of its aspects; and (3) dialogue is essential to living the Church's mission. This last belief was also central to the Council's deliberations. We recall how John XXIII desired that the Council throw open institutional windows so that the Church could see out, and people could see into the Church.[1] Similarly in 1964, as the Council was reconvening, Paul VI issued his first encyclical, *Ecclesiam suam*, in which he too spoke of the importance of dialogue. In fact, this was the first time the word *dialogue* was used in official Church teaching. Paul VI describes how dialogues are integral to the nature of the Church because God initiates a dialogue with humanity and continually speaks to us through Christ in the Holy Spirit. Offering a model of concentric circles of dialogue, Paul VI shows how these exchanges are more than a political strategy. Dialogue within the Catholic Church, with Christians, all religions, and civil society helps us learn how to make spiritual contact with others and therein create a foundation for authentic collaboration.

Looking at the subsequent discussions of the Council, especially those that focused on preparing a Statement on the Jews, and the final document discussed earlier, *Gaudium et spes*, we can see how this encyclical immediately bore fruit.

Nostra aetate (NA), the document on the relation of the Church to non-Christian religions, marks an evolutionary moment in interreligious dialogue by proclaiming that "the Catholic Church rejects nothing that is true and holy in these [non-Christian] religions" (no. 2). What began as an effort to create a statement about the Church's relationship with Judaism became a call for cooperation among all religions (NA 1). The Council deliberations that produced this document drew from the experiences of the bishops in the Middle East, Africa, and Asia. Their reports acknowledged the challenges faced by faith communities as they strive to live together peacefully in these contexts. This frank sharing emerged as a decisively positive claim acknowledging how all religions possess rays of truth for humankind and that Christians should acknowledge, preserve, and encourage the spiritual and moral truths within them (NA 2). In this claim, the Council identifies the movement of God's Spirit: "From ancient times down to the present, there is found among various peoples a certain perception of that hidden power which hovers over the course of things and over the events of human history" (no. 2).

The historical significance of this document is twofold. First, John Borelli notes that *Nostra aetate* represents the first time in the twenty universal councils of the Catholic Church that the Church actually encourages dialogue with Muslims.[2] It also brings to light how significant theological reflections on Islam have taken place throughout our history. Second, a new generation of documents emerged since the Council that offer a foundation for the development of bilateral dialogues. In particular, the documents of the Pontifical Council for Interreligious Relations—such as *Dialogue and Proclamation*, which marked the twenty-fifth anniversary of *Nostra aetate*—offered significant guidance for interreligious dialogue.

Insights from This Anniversary

The documents of the Second Vatican Council offer to the global community a vision of the common dignity of persons made in God's image. The Council has expanded our idea of church beyond institutional structures and has called us all to the service of humankind in ways that uphold and foster human dignity. The documents also point to ways in which interreligious dialogue can address real needs and problems in the world, and maintain that it is the Church's mission to engage in these dialogues. The Church's teachings guide these exchanges by offering theological and practical principles, all of which can foster a culture of dialogue with other religions. In these encounters, we discover God's grace at work in the world.

Over the last fifty years, the Church's engagement with interreligious dialogue has had some success. However, dialogue remains principally the work of institutional leaders and academics, even though service organizations such as Sant'Egidio and the Focolare movement have offered models for grassroots participation in dialogue. We need to help Catholics realize how interreligious dialogue is an integral part of their own identity and mission. For as Paul VI noted, God is the initiator of dialogue and God calls us to expand our dialogues within the Catholic Church, with other Christians and religions, and in all society. Training our communities in dialogue is especially critical today, given the decline in current public discourse. John Courtney Murray, who promoted such discourse in his writings, often spoke about the rise of barbarianism when rational discourse breaks down. He avers that "civility breaks down with the death of dialogue."[3] Moreover, entering into dialogue with Muslims, especially now with the current challenges regarding the perception of Islam in the world, is an important apostolic work of the Church.

Another area for growth is in devoting equal efforts to all types of dialogue. Where previous dialogues focused primarily on discussions of life, theological dialogues must also be embraced. We see this happening in the academic field of comparative theology and the gatherings of Christian and Muslim scholars for the A Common Word initiative. The Catholic Church has been a significant partner in these contexts. A critical next step requires formally incorporating interreligious learning into academic and pastoral training of Christian and Muslim scholars and community leaders. This will enhance theological study and improve relations between Christians and Muslims.

CONGREGATION OF THE SISTERS OF THE HOLY CROSS (1841–PRESENT)

The 175th Anniversary of the Congregation of the Sisters of the Holy Cross (CSC), founded in LeMans, France, in 1841, reveals important aspects of interreligious dialogue. Looking at our history, I see the many ways in which the family of Holy Cross religious and associates fostered dialogues and developed creative collaborations in various contexts. Our Constitutions state that our apostolic focus is to communicate in word and action God's desire for "the transformation of human hearts and human relationships."[4] In this mission statement we also acknowledge

> our own powerlessness and need for God's love, [relying] on the Spirit in opening ourselves to experience Christ's liberating salvation in and with the people we serve…[and that] our awareness of sin and its consequences in the world obliges us to examine our own lives to see to what depth we have assimilated the gospel message.[5]

Our Constitution also says that we communicate God's desire for this transformation by building up a society of justice and love. Our model is Mary, Mother of sorrows, "who, full of compassion for the world, stood courageously at the foot of the cross united with her son in the work of salvation."[6]

Committed to being a compassionate presence in the world, we united diverse communities to create a future together. In the spirit of our founder, Basil Moreau, we take risks, crossing borders of every sort. Our unity in Christ is the source of this courage. Moreau's favorite image was the vine and the branches (John 15:1–11), and he believed that attentiveness to the interior life with Christ would bear fruit for the world. Moreau also articulated how we were to "live together as close friends"[7] and that ministry flows from our understanding of a communion of persons in which all can learn and be enriched.[8] Friendships are a source of ongoing growth in charity and justice. Over the years we have become more deeply aware of the movement of God's spirit changing us both personally and communally.

Reflecting on This Anniversary

Reflecting on the Sisters of the Holy Cross 175th Anniversary and my experiences of ministry with the Christians and Muslims in Bangladesh and the United States, I believe our interactions were sacred conversations. Much like *lectio divina*, the process of reading, meditation, prayer, and contemplation, our interreligious encounters are dialogues wherein God's presence in one another is discovered. We recognize the movement of God's spirit in our common endeavors of education and other social outreach projects. Drawing from our intellectual and spiritual resources, our decision-making fostered an active solidarity as we promoted the common good for all people. As John XXIII noted in *Pacem in terris* (PT), this solidarity is "achieved by all kinds of mutual collaboration" (no. 98) and, in particular, brings together distinct ethnic contributions and spiritual values of various groups in societies (no. 100).

John XXIII's proposal foreshadows Hans Küng's famous statement: "There will be no peace among the nations without peace among the religions. There will be no peace among religions without dialogue among the religions," and the Global Ethics platform of the 1993 World Parliament of Religions written by Küng emphasizes a sense of urgency in promoting interreligious solidarity.[9] John XXIII focused on the moral authority of religions to contribute to securing human rights, sustaining positive relations among political and civil sectors, and therein promoting peace. Moreover, as Timothy Wright, a longtime partner in Monastic Interreligious Dialogues posits, there is no peace without prayer,[10] that is, openness to God's transformative presence. Contemplation is essential to our deliberations, especially in evaluating our decisions.

Examining the history of the Sisters of the Holy Cross and my own experiences, I see how this type of discernment fostered interreligious friendships. As we exchanged beliefs, ideals, and aspirations of one another's faith tradition, we developed greater solidarity with them. Today these friendships have also tutored us in a common call to a stewardship of Mystery. Together we have become caretakers of the gifts God's Spirit generously shares with us as interreligious and intercultural communities. Interreligious friendships keep us connected even in the midst of doubt and conflict. This steadfastness, like Mary's at the foot of the cross, is a manifestation of hope: a complete trust in God's loving plan for all creation. As our Holy Cross motto says, *O Crux, Ave Spes Unica.*

CONCLUSION

These two anniversaries with their historical contributions to interreligious relationships bring into focus two strands critical to the future of dialogue. First, our dialogues should bear witness that all people are created in God's image and strive to respond to God's grace. These endeavors do not undermine our religious beliefs. In fact, our affection for the faith makes these dialogues an experience of mutual fecundity. Our Catholic documents and guidelines indicate a commitment to interreligious learning. Additionally, the effectiveness of this learning occurs as participation expands to include local communities in these dialogues, and the study of one another's sacred texts becomes central to these discussions.

Some scholars contend that practical religious theories of social engagement are the principal resources for interreligious comparisons.[11] I believe, however, that the consideration of systematic or philosophical components of these theories are essential to discovering the deeper meanings of a religion's teachings. Engaging in a hermeneutical approach to sacred texts facilitates this important analysis and interaction. The goal of such dialogues and studies is not to minimize differences but to engage them with greater openness.

Where comparative studies are contextualized, culture, social location, and experience aid in the interpretation of sacred texts. Such scholarship serves a believer's faith and practice when shared with coreligionists and in interreligious settings; it builds social capital between local and academic communities based on shared interests, values, and aspirations. Finally, these projects generate enthusiasm for interreligious learning.

The second strand regarding the evolution of dialogue flows from the first. Dialogue and comparative studies are opportunities for spiritual growth in interreligious gatherings. Basil Moreau's plan was that Holy Cross brothers, priests, and sisters would become educators in the faith through their positive example in scholarship and the spiritual life. Our dialogues, in community and with others, reveal the ways this learning forms us in faith. Moreau mandates, the mind should "not be cultivated at the expense of the heart."[12] This model of interreligious learning, *educare*, brings forth the goodness God intends.[13] Dialogue then provides a forum for meeting other faiths, learning from them, and contemplating with them as we work for justice and support ways for our communities to flourish. In this learning, we grasp the varied ways God's spirit animates these encounters and the movements of our own hearts.

In the second part of this essay, I move from these recommendations to a fuller description of sacred conversations as opportunities to deepen faith and love in ways that foster harmony and comity among faiths and cultures. Sacred conversations are then journeys that can promote a spirituality of dialogue capable of addressing the historical burdens, ethical dilemmas, and theological impasses that emerge as religions meet face-to-face.

PART II

SACRED CONVERSATIONS

Sacred conversations foster a spirituality of dialogue that can enhance and expand interreligious learning among various groups in our faith communities. Thus dialogue will build a civilization of love, respecting the dignity of all persons. In Christianity and Islam specifically, this goal is expressed in the conviction that human beings are creatures who bear God's image (Gen 1:26) or breath (Qur'an 38:72), and they have a responsibility for this work. The recognition of this truth is the basis for Christians and Muslims to develop partnerships characterized by respect, reciprocity, and solidarity.[1] As the 2007 "A Common Word" letter from 138 Muslim global leaders and scholars to Christians throughout the world stated:

> Say: O People of the Scripture! Come to a common word between us and you: that we shall worship none but God, and that we shall ascribe no partner unto Him, and that none of us shall take others for lords beside God. And if they turn away, then say: Bear witness that we are they who have surrendered (unto Him). (Aal 'Imran 3:64)[2]

11

In this way, dialogue among Christians and Muslims reveals the depths of God's loving plan for all creation, because through them we learn how each faith tradition understands this plan in distinct as well as similar ways.

CATHOLIC CHRISTIANITY AND DIALOGUE

The Catholic Church's teachings about dialogue emerge from both the history of Christian relations with communities throughout the world and the desire for the Church to renew its commitment to serve humankind. The Church developed guidelines to help scholars and communities engage with other religions. *Dialogue and Proclamation* (DP) (1991), a document marking the twenty-fifth anniversary of *Nostra aetate*, emphasizes dialogue as part of the Church's evangelization and a means for growth in faith:

> Dialogue means "all positive and constructive interreligious relations with individuals and communities of other faiths which are directed at mutual understanding and enrichment," in obedience to truth and respect for freedom. It includes both witness and the exploration of respective religious convictions. (DP 9)

Dialogue and Proclamation also states that "the foundation of the Church's commitment to dialogue is not merely anthropological but primarily theological" (no. 38). This is the dialogue of salvation in which all people can realize that "God, in an age-long dialogue, has offered and continues to offer salvation to humankind" (no. 38). The aim, therefore, is a "deeper conversion of all towards God" (no. 41) as we respond "with increasing sincerity to God's personal call and gracious self-gift" made known to us in Christ and the work of his Spirit (no. 40).

Thus dialogue is a call to ever-deepening discipleship (DP 70) as Christians become more effective witnesses to Gospel truth (DP 55–57). This process is characterized by a balanced and open attitude and remains cognizant of the way in which insufficient grounding of one's own faith, lack of knowledge about religions, and suspicions about another's motives can become obstacles to dialogue (DP 47–55).

Dialogue and Proclamation also builds on the four forms of dialogue identified in the 1984 document *Dialogue and Mission*. These are dialogue of life, dialogue of action, dialogue of theological exchange, and dialogue of spiritual experiences. Together these dialogues lead to fruitful exchanges, especially when Catholics maintain confidence in the power of the Holy Spirit and respect for the Spirit's presence and action in these dialogues (DP 70).

Over the years, various organizations have helped to carry out these dialogues. Episcopal conferences, theological centers, and Catholic social service groups all have engaged in important dialogues. These efforts, especially in the 1990s, created networks for interreligious learning and cooperation, some of which remained active in academic circles with theological comparative studies and centers for theological formation. In fact, success accrued especially in Catholic and Muslim bilateral exchanges.[3] As John Borelli notes, however, the role of the institutional Catholic Church in these dialogues "has diminished in recent years," and the Muslim initiative A Common Word offers a means of refreshing interreligious dialogue in the Catholic Church.[4]

ISLAM AND DIALOGUE

Muslims throughout the world engaged with various religious communities dating back to the time of Muhammad. Islamic history illustrates how dialogic encounters with Jews and Christians focused largely on inviting them to Islam. However, documentation also reveals how Jewish and Christian communities allied themselves with Muslim communities for protection against religious persecution.

John Andrew Morrow has recently published important research on these alliances. "The Covenants Project" explores letters and treaties during the Prophet's time that established these accords.[5] The project conducts rigorous study of the sociopolitical history and provides a critical resource for Islamic teaching about interreligious and intercultural relations. The research indicates how Muslims understood their call to be just stewards of God's creation, including the care and protection of all communities in a given geographic area.

In addition, the eight-volume work *Christian-Muslim Relations: A Bibliographical History* surveys these relationships from 600 through the 1800s.[6] It is an important resource for understanding the interactions, attitudes about, and knowledge of each other during these periods and the way these exchanges contributed to the social history of both traditions.

Both studies, moreover, show how Muslims understood their commitment to foster productive relationships with others. The Qur'an offers guidance for these dialogues and engagements. The Qur'an says that exchanges with others should foster understanding (*ta'aruf*, 49:13) and facilitate bridge-building/reconciliation (*islah*, 4:114) by using wise and goodly exhortation (*al-hikmah wa al-maw'izat al-hasanah*, 16:125).[7] Islamic tradition also conveys how Prophet Muhammad is a model for dialogue by "maintaining peaceful coexistence with his enemies and respect for their religions and beliefs. He promoted freedom of thought and free expression in preaching."[8] His beliefs and behavior reminds Muslims that they are "to become people of forbearance, wisdom, caring, and justice" for all "regardless of race, genders, color or religion."[9]

Organizations such as Bangladesh Rural Advancement Committee (BRAC), Salam Institute for Justice and Peace, and the Islamic Networks Group promote interreligious exchanges in the spirit of Muhammad and Islamic teachings. In addition, as noted earlier, the 2007 A Common Word initiative in which Muslims from a large number of countries, including academics, politicians, writers, and muftis, suggest new opportunities for deepening interreligious understanding and cooperation between Christians and Muslims. The invitation letter to this program states,

Muslims and Christians together make up well over half of the world's population. Without peace and justice between these two religious communities, there can be no meaningful peace in the world. The future of the world depends on peace between Muslims and Christians.

The basis for this peace and understanding already exists. It is part of the very foundational principles of both faiths: love of the One God, and love of the neighbour. These principles are found over and over again in the sacred texts of Islam and Christianity. The Unity of God, the necessity of love for Him, and the necessity of love of the neighbour is thus *the common ground* between Islam and Christianity.[10]

Over the last nine years, Christians and Muslims have joined together to explore sacred texts. These dialogues produced various types of publications and courses for academic study on interreligious relations. The concluding document of the November 2008 seminar of the Catholic-Muslim forum, sponsored by the Pontifical Council for Interreligious Dialogue and the Royal Al-Bayt Institute in Amman, recommits the religions to building a civilization of love:

> We profess that Catholics and Muslims are called to be instruments of love and harmony among believers, and for humanity as a whole, renouncing any oppression, aggressive violence and terrorism, especially that committed in the name of religion, and upholding the principles of justice for all.[11]

This initiative reminds us that Catholic and Islamic traditions have a history of interaction that extends beyond social exchange to rigorous study of one another's sacred texts, all of which inform just actions. Furthermore, this history offers models for ways to discover holiness in these sacred teachings. Interreligious dialogue will expand and deepen to build a civilization of love as our religions develop a spirituality of dialogue attentive to movements of God's Spirit. Sacred conversation is a means for cultivating this spirituality.

SACRED CONVERSATIONS

Sacred conversations are interreligious dialogues and studies devoted to deep learning about God, that is, God's active presence in our own faith and action as well as in our partner's tradition. These conversations honor the integrity of religious traditions, especially by recognizing syncretistic tendencies in interpreting religious teachings and practices. The common ground becomes a shared experience of witnessing to God's transformational action in a believer's life. These interreligious encounters manifest the holiness of persons and faith communities as they strive to live their faith authentically.

Open to the movement of Spirit, sacred conversations echo Bernard Lonergan's transcendental method: "Be attentive, intelligent, reasonable, and responsible."[12] These conversations align with Lonergan's idea of conversion, which reveals self-transcending qualities of human beings[13] and the capacity for intersubjectivity facilitating the discovery of meaning, especially in the "lives and deeds of others."[14] The three dimensions of conversion are the intellectual, moral, and religious.[15] Sacred conversations reveal ways to experience personally

God's call to ever-deepening faith and love, a conversion of mind and heart through *contemplative endeavors*, *creative freedom*, and *evolutionary consciousness* experienced as movements of God's grace in our lives.

Sacred conversations are *contemplative endeavors* that help us to become steadfast students of cultures and religions. In these engagements, we are attentive to both differences and similarities in religious teachings and practices. Keeping such "learning in the forefront," these analogues enhance our respect for one another's traditions and shape theological imaginations.[16] Sacred conversations can lead believers to an intellectual conversion by overcoming naïve realism, idealism, conceptualism, relativism, and romanticism concerning other religious beliefs and practices. Lonergan points out that "intellectual conversion is a radical clarification and, consequently, the elimination of an exceedingly stubborn and misleading myth concerning reality, objectivity, and human knowledge."[17] As sacred conversations devote energies to deep listening and feedback about knowledge shared, participants will address the misinformation about religions readily available to each religion. Thus, these engagements help each one's growth in faith. According to psychologist James Fowler, believers often remain in the conventional stage of faith development by not critically examining their beliefs.[18] Exposure to different ideas transcends the comfort zone of being "inside the institutional system" so as to grasp religious truths as "powerful forces" underlying our knowing.[19]

Sacred conversations lead to experiences of *creative freedom*. Taking responsibility for interreligious learning, the participants recognize various religious perspectives offering significant insights about God, creation, and humankind, including the concerns and aspirations of particular groups. Connections between these views and the values they express become normative. The encounters foster greater self-understanding and animate our discernment and decision-making. Thus sacred conversations facilitate our moral conversion.

These dialogues commit those engaged to pursuing true objective values that overcome conventional or personal preference. Lonergan explains the process: "As our knowledge of human reality increases, as our responses to human values are strengthened and refined, our mentors more and more leave us to ourselves so that our freedom may exercise its ever advancing thrust toward authenticity."[20] This active solidarity was described in part 1. Solidarity connects with movements in the Catholic Church such as JustFaith[21] and the Muslim community's Salam Justice and Peace Institute, which sees spiritual-moral formation as a critical component to works of justice.

Sacred conversations are holy/holistic dialogues. They gracefully embrace a freedom to be known by religious others. Those engaged learn to appreciate, even love, these connections as God loves them. We develop interreligious friendships capable of holding in esteem the mystery of God's active presence in creation. The connections lead to an *evolutionary consciousness* borne as we remain open to God's call to new depths of faith and love, greater authenticity, and a religious conversion.[22] In this modality of self-transcendence, God's love floods hearts through the Holy Spirit and becomes the ongoing dynamic of cooperation with God and others.

A lack of generosity undermines this conversion. Thomas Aquinas, in his study of the virtue of charity, says that "it is more proper to charity to desire to love than to desire being loved."[23] Sacred conversations nurture this generous love necessary for religious conversion.

"Religious conversion is to a total being-in-love as the efficacious ground of all self-transcendence, whether in pursuit of truth, or the realization of human values, or in the orientation man [sic] adopts to the universe, its ground, and its goal."[24] Grasped by ultimate concern, converts seek ways to promote a future larger than themselves, that is, communicating in word and deed God's desire for the transformation of human hearts and relationships in a religiously complex world. Thus they can deepen respect and love for other faith traditions.

These three aspects of sacred conversations undergird a variety of dialogues, including interdisciplinary, intercultural, and interreligious. As such, these conversations become as Carl Jung described: a "spiritual adventure—the exposure of human consciousness to the undefined and the indefinable."[25] These journeys are

[a] passing over and coming back…experimenting with the truth of life and death. In passing over to other lives, one is led to turn the truth of one's own life into poetry. This is especially clear when one comes to the point of saying to oneself, "You are what (hu)man is" and "You are what God is." Still the poetry here is not a falsification of the truth; it embodies rather deeper insight into the truth. Passing over to other lives changes one's understanding of what (hu)man is and who God is.[26]

These crossings shape a spirituality of dialogue rooted in strong faith and just action. Christians and Muslims have valuable resources for these journeys. These resources align with recent studies concerning interreligious dialogue and methods for comparative theological study.

RESOURCES FOR SACRED CONVERSATIONS

Sacred conversations nurture a spirituality of dialogue. Teachings of religious traditions and studies about dialogue provide resources for these conversations. The first set consists of the ethical teachings of religious traditions. The second set represents recent studies concerning dialogue in academic and social settings. I will explore both sets of resources using my experiences with Christian and Muslim communities.

THEOLOGICAL VIRTUE IN CHRISTIANITY AND ISLAM

The entry point for ethical considerations for Muslims and Christians is reflection on the question, "As a believer, how ought I to live?" The Christian response to this question recognizes that God calls believers to an ongoing and deepening commitment to Christ and the unfolding of God's kingdom. Muslims respond to this question by striving to remain faithful servants of God and stewards of creation. The virtue theories that emerge from these commitments focus on character formation as deepening faith in and love for God and for others. In their writings on ethics, Thomas Aquinas and Abu Hamid Al-Ghazali each offer this guidance according to their respective traditions, and these can serve as motivations and resources for sacred conversations, especially when examining the teleological nature of their virtue theory, the types of virtues they identify, and the way these virtues foster personal and social transformation.

The teleological nature of Aquinas's and Ghazali's ethics describes the final goal of perfect happiness with God and the ways this goal animates the moral life in this life and the next, in themselves and in others. Reflection on this goal, beatitude (*beatitudo*) or the real blessedness (*as-Saʿada al-Haqiqiya*), unifies and transforms human thoughts, desires, and actions. In this way, Aquinas and al-Ghazali maintain that authentic human flourishing depends on possession of virtues to guide them toward perfect happiness, while enjoying earthly knowledge and love of God.[27] As an ongoing process of formation, both thinkers emphasize how character formation relies on the believer's openness to God's initiatives.

CHRISTIANITY

Aquinas's ethical theory posts two basic categories of virtues: the acquired and the infused. The acquired virtues consist of intellectual and moral virtues. He further divides the intellectual virtues into two groups: the speculative and practical. The speculative comprises three: understanding, science (a habit of conclusions), and wisdom (ST I-II 57.2),[28] and the practical two: art (*ars*) and prudence (ST I-II 57.3 ad 4). The speculative virtues consider truth itself (ST I-II 57.1), while the practical guides human choice (ST I-II 57.4). Aquinas describes the connection between these virtues, showing how they foster a believer's ability to grasp truth, use reason, and judge (ST I-II 57.2). Wisdom is the perfection of all these three powers because with it persons possess knowledge of the highest cause (ST II-II 45.1).

In Aquinas's theory, moral virtues shape the will and the appetitive part of reason. Justice regards the rightness of action in external relations between people and guides believers to promote the common good. Courage and temperance help in ordering the passions. Practical right reason, or prudence in Aquinas's theory, perfects moral and intellectual virtue by applying right reason to action in accordance with the appropriate mean of these actions (ST I-II 64.1), and here the virtue of prudence is key (ST I-II 65.1).

Aquinas's virtue theory includes a discussion about the relationships between infused virtues and acquired virtue. The latter facilitates the performance of determined right actions toward specific proper ends; infused virtues provide competencies enabling believers to reach their most fitting and ultimate end, perfect happiness (ST I-II 63.3 ad 2). Aquinas lists two kinds of infused virtue: theological, "supernatural virtues per se;" and the moral virtues, "per accidens." God confers these virtues directly through the gift of grace (ST I-II 55.4 ad 6). The theological virtues faith, hope, and charity dispose the human will to God's direction (ST I-II 62.1; 65.5). Faith provides the knowledge that arouses desire for God and hope strives toward God. Faith assents to revealed truths, greater than the mind can grasp or imagine, and knowledge moving the person "inwardly by grace" (ST II-II 6.1). Hope enables believers to cooperate with grace, aids them in overcoming obstacles, and fosters a steadfast turning toward supernatural happiness with God (ST II-II 17.6 ad 3). Charity perfects faith and hope and all virtues, because this virtue is the "mother and root of all virtues...directing all acts to their last end" (ST I-II 62.4; II-II 23.8).

Faith, hope, and charity are the seeds for the second type of infused virtue, the moral virtues. Infused prudence, justice, courage, and temperance make humans good citizens with the saints and members of God's household (ST I-II 63.4). Social actions are more perfect, that is, corresponding to beatitudes (ST I-II 63.3). Charity, as Servais Pinckaers explains, "touches and organizes [all] the virtues," without replacing "the proper action of each and every virtue."[29]

Aquinas's ethics draws upon the interconnections between law and grace, especially exploring how the gifts and fruits of the Holy Spirit and the gospel beatitudes contribute to moral goodness. Aquinas believes these gifts help persons to become habitually receptive to guidance of the Holy Spirit (ST I-II 68.6).

In his explanation of charity, Aquinas outlines how believers can increase in virtue.[30] He illustrates the importance of acquired intellectual or moral virtues in the process and the ways God's love moves persons to greater freedom, a freedom for excellence in reasoning, feeling, and execution of the will.[31] Moving from the beginners' stage to the progressives, and finally to the "perfecti," each phase guides believers to see how God calls them to greater love and freedom:

[They] are led through patient acceptance of trials and obstacles, to the fulfillment of a life project, which gives meaning, value, and fruitfulness to existence. The perfection of moral freedom is shown by the response to vocation, by devotion to a great cause, however humble it may appear to be, or the accomplishment of important tasks in the service of one's community, family, city, or Church.[32]

Far from lessening human freedom, each stage of moral development leads believers toward greater authenticity and excellence. Thus, Aquinas's teachings point to the need for a believer's ongoing growth, as growth is critical to Christians' response to life in church and society.

ISLAM

Al-Ghazali teaches that believers must develop a beautiful character (*husn al-khuluq*) by cultivating right knowledge (*ilm*), good action (*amal*)—also understood as right activity (*islam*)—religious intelligence (*iman*), and ethical integrity (*ihsan*). These teachings from the Hadith of Jibreel narrate the essence of religion as moral excellence.[33]

Al-Ghazali's ethics describes how believers perfect their character by acquiring virtue (*fadilah*). Virtues are developed through learning, habituation, and God's assistance.[34] The process includes the use of reason (*aql*), which aids in understanding revealed teachings and the shaping of desires (*hawa*). Central here is the integration of the three domains (mentioned earlier) in ways fostering greater attentiveness to God (*taqwa*), which, in turn, helps believers balance needs, concerns, and duties of everyday life according to this goal.[35]

Al-Ghazali's writings describe three basic categories of virtue: the philosophical, religious-legal, and mystical.[36] The philosophical virtues of wisdom (include here prudence), temperance, and fortitude help believers to balance the various powers or appetites of the human soul. The "right balance" struck by practicing these virtues is the means for acquiring justice. The religious virtues are divine guidance (*hidayah*), good counsel (*rushd*), direction (*tasdid*), and support (*ta'yid*). They are, in his theory, theological virtues drawing believers nearer to God by means of God's grace. Accordingly, they facilitate a believer's adherence to spiritual duties (*ibadat*) and social responsibilities (*adat*).[37]

In explaining mystical virtues, al-Ghazali draws from the tradition of Sufi teachers concerning "stations" of spiritual perfection. The first virtue is repentance (*tauba*); with this virtue, the wayfarer progresses to the highest virtue, love (*mahabbah*). Al-Ghazali also lists five mystical virtues necessary for this progress: greater resolve or intention (*niyyah*), sincerity (*ikhlas*), truthfulness (as related to resolution; *'azm*), vigilance (*muraqabah*), and meditation (*tafakkur*). These provide capacities for deeper intimacy with God and further moral-spiritual growth.

Growth in moral character follows a trajectory much like the pattern al-Ghazali adopts for his major work *Ihya ulum-aldin*. The structure of the *Ihya* contains four major sections. Each section serves as a stage in a spiritual-moral itinerary that leads to greater awareness of God and nearness to God. The first two books in the first section identify the hermeneutic for discovering the essential elements of moral-spiritual development. Through knowledge and faith, a believer comes to realize the inner dimensions of worship and ethical actions. The inner dimension consists of mindfulness of God, a deeper God-consciousness (*taqwa*). The rest of the books in the first and second sections (quarters 1 and 2) describe in detail how this occurs in a believer's personal growth in faith and interaction with others. The model for perfect action in faith and practice is Prophet Muhammad, the topic of the final book in the second section.

The final sections, third and fourth quarters, of the *Ihya* outline the intensification of this journey to deeper faith. In fact, al-Ghazali's introduction states that the pattern of his study is modeled on "the science of revelation and practical religion," both directed to an "alchemy of happiness"—focusing on knowledge of God, self, this world, and the next[38] that changes the heart to become a subtle substance open to Divine Assistance. Al-Ghazali offers guidance for cultivating greater God-consciousness (*taqwa*) to keep the heart ready to respond to God and the needs of others.

As noted above, ideas concerning moral formation can be effective resources for promoting the sacred conversations between Muslims and Christians. Learning how faith communities envision holistic personal development serves the common good but also offers insights about a religious tradition's priorities. Persons made in God's image, or in the "best of molds," have both a temporal and transcendent end, and move toward this goal as a realization and promotion of this good in the world. Seeking nearness to God and fostering the common good tutors believers in learning how to remain in this truth and act from this truth. Christian and Muslim ethical teachings provide a resource for recognizing that, as believers, God calls us to ever-deepening faith and love. Life in this world and the next is a continual journey to God and the realization of greater freedom and authenticity.

Muslims and Christians, who believe God is the source, summit, and sustainer of all, learn to act knowingly, lovingly, and generously with all because of their love for God and all others in God. Both traditions highlight ways in which God's Spirit moves believers toward cultivating virtue not only for themselves but for the good of all society. Sacred conversations can deepen this awareness personally, communally, and across traditions. Moreover, these virtue theories are powerful resources for realizing intrinsic motivations to engage in sacred conversations.

CONTEMPORARY VIRTUE THEORY AND DIALOGUE

Dialogue and intertextual studies as described by theologians and philosophers identify ways in which this process connects to intellectual, moral, and theological virtue. These studies emphasize the importance of dialogue and its possible evolution beyond social cordiality in order to promote interreligious learning and friendship.

In *Virtues in Dialogue: Belief, Religious Diversity and Women's Interreligious Dialogue*, Mara Brecht offers an epistemological model she calls "Virtuous-Doxastic [belief-forming] Practice (VDP)."[39] Using a case study of a women's interreligious dialogue group in Pennsylvania, she finds that believers form and justify their convictions through the exercise of intellectual virtues that are "socially motivated and socially significant toward promoting social flourishing."[40]

Brecht lists four epistemic virtues—steadfastness, judiciousness, prudence, and creativity—and two meta-level epistemic virtues—intellectual integrity and wisdom. The intellectual virtues serve as navigational tools regulating belief formation in a pluralistic and complex world[41] and highlight how dialogue can enhance personal transformation. Particularly helpful is the way Brecht connects temperance to steadfastness, describing it as "a quality of how the agent holds what she believes." Steadfastness empowers faithfulness to one's own tradition while exploring another's. It also enables persons to remain in the process of dialogue during difficult or confusing points of the exchange.

Frank Clooney's model of comparative theology is a good example of steadfastness in formal study. In *Comparative Theology: Deep Learning across Religious Borders*, Clooney describes intertextual reading as "a practical response to religious diversity read with our eyes open, interpreting the world in light of our faith and with a willingness to see newly the truth of our own religion in light of another."[42] He also notes that this type of reading can occur with traditions not formally textual-based, and that it is good to "keep comparative theology and interreligious dialogue closely connected."[43] This intertextual reading requires at least six qualities: reverence for the text, care and loving attention, keeping our biases in check, more listening than judging, patient study, and sensitivity in offering commentary. It is a thoughtful reading of sacred texts, not a consuming of religious writings.[44] Clooney claims these "cross-readings are religious as well as scholarly acts and should be performed in that spirit."[45]

The Church of England's *Building Bridges Seminars* (2002–13) offers another example, devoted as it is to promoting interreligious learning between Muslims and Christians.[46] Professor Asma Afsaruddin, my colleague and responder to this lecture, participated in these dialogues. Sessions took place in various Christian and Islamic centers around the world. The goal of these conversations was clearly stated by Prince El Hassan bin Talal of Jordan: "Difference was not seen as a threat, but as a reality; it was not a route to degeneration, but to renewal."[47] The organization and the topics of the seminars attested to this insight. They provided a study of sacred texts, prophecy, theological anthropology, secularism, modernity, role of religion in society, the relationships between religion and science, justice and peace, human rights, the common good, prayer, and teachings about death and resurrection.

In these dialogues, participants engaged the complexity and diversity of their own traditions, raising questions and sharing insights openly, honestly, and self-critically. Moreover, as former Archbishop of Canterbury Rowan Williams noted, these exchanges became opportunities to "watch each other" engaging with their sacred texts. In this way, dialogues are "fundamentally oriented toward getting to know one another's hearts."[48] Developing intellectual virtues, as exhibited in these intertextual studies, points to the importance of engaging philosophical or theological resources that undergird these texts. Cultivating intellectual virtues contributes vitally to understanding sacred traditions by fostering ongoing learning in the dialogue process. Ideally, these virtues promote the intellectual conversion described above by enabling our sacred conversations to deeply ponder different ideas and beliefs. These considerations lead to moral and religious conversion; however, it requires the cultivation of moral and theological virtue, as described in the ethics of Aquinas and al-Ghazali.

In *Impossibility of Interreligious Dialogue*, Catherine Cornille observes that "the very urgency with which religions are called to engage in peaceful and constructive conversations may in fact signal a certain religious reticence, if not resistance, to dialogue."[49] Claiming that "the main obstacle for dialogue is not so much outside as within religious traditions," she describes five conditions critical for dialogue: humility, commitment, interconnection, empathy, and hospitality.[50] Cornille explores how these conditions "apply to all forms of intercultural and interreligious hermeneutics,"[51] and nurture a capacity to learn from other religions. In addition to a discussion of intellectual virtue, her study also points to the need to develop moral virtue for dialogue. Moral virtue motivates the will to know the good and choose it. Her study of humility and hospitality points to a critical need to this shaping of the will for dialogue and the importance of prudential judgment.

Humility in dialogue guides the other conditions for dialogue that Cornille identifies—commitment, interconnectedness, and empathy. With humility, dialogue guides the journey from our own tradition to another's and back *responsibly*, to promote *God's justice* in the world, and to deepen *compassion* for another by respecting differences, recognizing limitations, and remaining steadfast in the common pursuit of truth. Similarly, hospitality as a metacondition or virtue is the fruit or the "crown" of these conditions by sustaining a reflection of the self as guest and host in the multifaith contexts.[52] Humility and hospitality help dialogue partners to remain open to the possibility of genuine interreligious engagement of ideas, concerns, or aspirations and the values they represent. They facilitate sacred conversations and nurture the possibility for moral conversion: a maturing of our knowledge of the good and ability to promote the good.

James L. Fredericks's writing on interreligious friendship as a theological virtue represents another critical study concerning the formation needed for sacred conversation.[53] He believes that by developing friendships that "reach across the boundaries of doctrine, experience, and value," Christians can come to grasp diversity theologically, while also addressing this diversity "creatively and responsibly" in their own lives.[54] These relationships reveal God's presence. Fredericks's study buttresses my own convictions about the ways sacred conversations foster religious conversion, that is, the "total being-in-love, the efficacious ground of self-transcendence."[55] Motivated by God's love for us, and our love for others in God, these relationships nurture capabilities for contemplation and action in diverse and complex contexts.

Examples of interreligious exchanges of such spiritual masters as Bede Griffiths illustrate how persons can nurture interreligious friendships with a whole religious tradition. Bede devoted his life and writings to exploring a relationship with Hinduism. Having discovered God's presence in his experiences of Hinduism in India, he befriended the religion. He cultivated this friendship through a rigorous and generous study of Hindu teachings and worship. He deepened this knowledge by incorporating them into Christian thinking and spiritual practice. The care with which he took in befriending Hinduism serves as an example for ways that formal learning and experience with the worship practices of a religious tradition blossoms into deep respect and affection for a tradition.

Bede also created a place for meditation and learning in Tamil Nadu that serves to introduce others to his "friend," that is, engaging others in a sacred conversation with Hinduism. He recognized the difficulty of such encounters because they require a matured faith so as to recognize similarity and difference between one's own tradition and that of the partner of the dialogue. With sharp precision he admires the concept of God in Hinduism while also critiquing Hindu doctrines such as *samsara* or reincarnation. In *The Marriage of East and West*, Bede identifies ways in which the meetings between these two "worlds" is a fulfillment of each.[56] Moreover, these encounters can reveal to Christians God's presence in Hinduism and the fulfillment of the cosmic covenant in Christ.[57]

Thomas Merton's life and writings portray another example of befriending faith traditions. His studies of the spiritual teachings of Buddhism and Islam revealed to him ways in which the traditions could inform the contemplative life.[58] He introduced his Trappist brothers and all Christians to the meditative practices of these traditions and opened doors for a deeper experience of Buddhism and Sufism.[59] Friendships fostered by sacred conversations are ways for believers to deepen their faith by remaining open to and cooperating with God's movement.

These resources point to the formation needed for Christians and Muslims to engage in sacred conversations. Remaining open to the movement of God's Spirit remains central to these dialogues. In the ethical traditions of Islam and Christianity, God's guidance keeps believers present to God's call to deeper conversion. As such, personal and social discernment remains in the forefront, as believers discover intrinsic motivation for dialogue in order to promote respect, reciprocity, and solidarity among their communities.

A spirituality of dialogue elicits newness wherein relationship to all life becomes the possibility that we "must embrace…re-patterning our institutions for cooperation and co-creativity."[60] Sacred conversations "create greater levels of connection, care, self-expression and creativity."[61] They emerge as the common enterprise that Teilhard described as a "zest for life, zest for living," in the "the dynamic processes of becoming."[62]

CONCLUSION:
SACRED CONVERSATIONS AS RELIGIOUS SUPERCOOPERATION?

The analysis thus far indicates how sacred conversations form a spirituality of dialogue by embracing religious and cultural diversity. It is with hope that dialogue partners remain open to discovering the interconnectedness of all creation in God and the possibility for future and greater cooperation among species—in other words, the *evolutionary* dimension. The motivation and practice of sacred conversation can also draw inspiration from the scientific concept of "supercooperation" in evolution theory.

Evolutionary theory identifies three general movements: *emergence*, *differentiation*, and *integration*. Scientists identify such principles as selection, adaptation, and mutation in these processes. Evolutionary biologist Martin Nowak's research describes how the principle of cooperation is the "master architect of evolution."[63] This principle of coresponsibility/coresponsiveness toward coevolution describes the willingness of species and subspecies to become "Super-Cooperators." Through features such as direct and indirect reciprocity, species seek paths that are a decision for growth even to the point of self-sacrifice. Evolution "needs" cooperation, he argues, in order to construct new levels of creative and innovative organization, for example, "driving genes to collaborate in chromosomes, chromosomes to collaborate in genomes, genomes to collaborate in cells, cells to collaborate in more complex cells, complex cells to collaborate in bodies, and bodies to collaborate in societies."[64]

Using an example of how language evolved and brought about innovative developments of the human species, Nowak's study illustrates how human cooperation uses each and every type of mechanism of cooperative interaction to a remarkable degree. He highlights how human brain development differs remarkably from "any other biological structure"[65] and that conversation is the distinctive mechanism to bring about this change and growth in the brain. Nowak says, "The next time you listen to another person, remember that you have permanently changed the wiring of your brain and will do this every time you memorize a moment no matter how fleeting."[66]

Recognizing this breathtakingly cooperative feature of human society, he notes that "the effort to wage war can be seen as a perverted form of cooperation" and that humans are "teetering on the brink of several catastrophes."[67] Given the fragility of intelligent life, Nowak warns that now more than ever "we need to cooperate, and on a global scale."[68] I believe this warning points to the need for multilayered dialogues and consultations, for sacred conversations. Ongoing learning and contemplations of the interconnectedness among persons, communities, and cosmos give rise to a will for self-donation and supercooperation. Each step of the evolutionary process requires cooperation and participation. Sacred conversation is a *decision* for such growth, for evolution.

Focusing on the importance of the evolutionary process, Alan Watkins has developed a theory to address the multifaceted nature of global problems he terms as "wicked." In the book he coauthored with social thinker and philosopher Ken Wilber, *Wicked and Wise: How to Solve the World's Toughest Problems*, he discusses the nature of these problems and offers "wise" ways to break through intractable concerns such as climate change, global militancy, and the confrontations within and among religions and cultures.[69] Watkins develops an "integral frame mapping" to emphasize the need for greater perception and dialogue in problem solving.[70] A deepening awareness of the multidimensional nature of wicked problems, especially the ways they consistently change, requires persons to be more attentive to subjective and objective dimensions of the individual and society at the heart of these concerns and behind proposed solutions.[71] With Watkins's and Wilber's work in mind, the movements that Nowak identifies as "cooperation" and the interior dimensions of dialogue identified here as sacred conversation become central to involving multistakeholders in multitiered, multichanneled, and multiorganizational efforts to create wise solutions.

Therefore if interdisciplinary, intercultural, and interreligious dialogues are to become sacred conversations and not just occasional luminous experiences, we must "learn how to become a learner."[72] Bringing a greater intentionality, honesty, and openness to God's spirit transforms these dialogues into sacred conversations. Sacred conversations are journeys embarked upon from one tradition to another and back, no matter the complexity or difficulty. A spirituality of dialogue remains open to conversion or liminality, that is, "growth and risk at the cutting edges," according to Diarmuid O'Murchu, a "fluidity, flexibility, creativity, and courageous abandonment to divine recklessness."[73]

The decision to dialogue with others becomes a tremendous commitment because individuals change in these exchanges. Sacred conversations, with their focus on the interior aspects of dialogue and the movements of the Spirit, do not fear these changes. In fact, sacred conversations foster the intellectual, moral, and spiritual growth critical to the "wicked" or complex and diverse religious and cultural realities in the world today.

PART III

SACRED CONVERSATIONS IN CONTEXT

In this part, I will offer three examples of sacred conversations that foster interreligious learning and enhance programs dedicated to this evolution of dialogue. The first example describes the Congregation of Holy Cross's ministry with Muslims in Bangladesh. The second features developments occurring in theological schools and academic centers. The third discusses religious and social organizations that promote interreligious networking.

HOLY CROSS IN BANGLADESH

The narrative of the Congregation of Holy Cross in Bangladesh offers an example of the ways a spirituality of dialogue promotes deep interreligious learning. For over one hundred years, Holy Cross remains committed to sacred conversations and the friendships that result from them. These relationships, like those fostered in other global contexts in which Holy Cross ministers, are a witness of hope, especially in times of great religious, social, and political conflict.

From 1852 to the present in Bangladesh, the Holy Cross congregations have encountered a complex and culturally rich society that "never really believed in shaking off past traditions or the values of the various religious codes."[1] They inherited not only this social history but also a complex Church history, since other diocesan priests and religious congregations of men and women had served the Christian populations.[2]

Challenges occurred in all phases of life and ministry, even to the point of doubting the mission itself. Like many other congregations, the purpose of missionary endeavors came under scrutiny during such trials. One important aspect of Holy Cross's presence during its early phases was a commitment to learning, and trials presented the greatest opportunities for learning. Through these trials, Holy Cross formed a deeper community within itself as well as with religious others. The initiatives in the cities of Chittagong and Dhaka, as well as throughout the villages, focused on preaching and teaching.[3] Mastering the Bengali language facilitated these ministries as missionaries connected with various village communities, chatting on mud verandas, learning from the stories shared by the people. These accounts revealed direct knowledge about religions in addition to grasping the social and political situation of the country. Throughout these encounters, Holy Cross communities encountered Advaita, an Asian theological principle of nonduality, which fosters an ability to live with difference and see the richness therein.

Learning to be students of the cultures and religions led to forming partnerships with various groups in Bangladesh. As the mission unfolded, Holy Cross sought collaborative ventures with various groups of Christian, Muslim, Hindu, Jain, Buddhist, and Tribal communities. This dialogue of life led to a sharing of common works. Presence to the immediate concerns of the people meant including them in consultations and decision-making as each sought to make a contribution to the future growth of the country. One significant example occurred in 1971 during the nine-month war fought by East Pakistan for independence from West Pakistan. In many parts of the country, Holy Cross protected and offered medical care for villagers and refugees, no matter their religion or side of the conflict. Holy Cross's stance for religious tolerance and respect for all people aligned with those planning for the new nation, Bangladesh, and a constitution that guarantees religious freedom.[4]

Holy Cross founder Basil Moreau's theory of education underscores these cooperative efforts, that education "flows from our understanding of a communion of persons in which all can learn and be enriched,"[5] as well as the Qur'anic teaching *ta 'aruf* that God created different nations and tribes so that they might seek each other's friendship and learn from each other's differences (Q 49:13). Thus in these partnerships, friendships flourished. Reverence for God's presence among us helped deconstruct false images of ourselves and others while we continually learned about and from one another.[6] With each new generation of endeavors, the conversations contributed a greater openness and honesty that helped us to recognize the movements of the Spirit in our common life and work. These friendships helped the Holy Cross community to experience the faith of the Bangladeshi people more intimately. Friendships ponder Mystery as Saint Paul explicates in 1 Corinthians 4:1–2.[7]

They cultivate a contemplative attitude for a boundary-crossing ministry that fosters respect and affection for other faith traditions, as we see in such models as Bede Griffiths and Thomas Merton. Friends learn how to wait, watch, and listen together for God. Thus, attentive to God's Spirit, interreligious friendships honor the goodness of all existence, the beauty of our interconnection with others, and the common call to foster a vision larger than ourselves.

In Islam, the corollary understanding comes into view with the concept of *taqwa* (God-consciousness) because as we see our actions and relationships, we recall God's presence with us, as noted in the instruction of *ihsan* in the *Hadith of Jibreel*, that is, doing the beautiful by remembering God in all things.[8] My friend of over thirty years expresses this understanding of *ihsan* as she examines the way friendship deepens as a virtue enabling us to become stewards of Mystery:

> If my friendship with Marianne is chosen by God, then it is our destiny to be friends, to appreciate and to give comfort and love to one another. In this way, our friendship contributes to the quality of life in our faith communities and cultures.
>
> These ideas remind me of the Sufi teachings of Maulana Rumi, Al Mansur, and Rabia Basri. The Sufis also advocated love as a means to reach their beloved "God." To them, the search for one's beloved transcends religions, class, and nations. Anyone can practice love, humility, and charity towards their companions to come closer to the ultimate goal—God who is All Love. To achieve bliss in this life, one

has to be tolerant, forgiving, and kind; one must pray and ask for God's mercy. Only the deserving achieve bliss/ecstasy/oneness with God. My friendship with Marianne is an opening to experience blessings from God and helps me to realize how these blessings can be shared with others.[9]

To ponder, to do the beautiful, requires an ongoing commitment to various types of sacred conversations. These conversations remain open to the Spirit, even in the midst of social crisis, because participants commit to collaborative discernment and action. As a recent NCR report on Global Sisters describes, Holy Cross Sisters continue to empower women through education and the promotion of interfaith understanding. When NCR asked, "Are there challenges in an environment in which conservative Islam is being felt more and more?" Sr. Violet Rodriguez replied,

Our constitution speaks of secularism as the foundation for our society, and I think that's a good thing, definitely. As for the environment at the school, we still think it is important for us, as educators, to emphasize the importance of respect for all religions—Islam, Buddhism, Hinduism and Christianity.[10]

More recently, after the brutal attacks of bloggers, attacks on foreign workers, and the July 1, 2016, rampage at the Holey Artisan Bakery cafe in Dhaka, leaders of the country are seeking ways to promote dialogue as a solution. In the summer of 2016, the District Commissioners of Bangladesh met to draw up recommendations and guidelines for addressing terrorism in the country. As Home Minister Asaduzzaman Khan Kamal reported, the meeting's agenda focused on creating "specific directives" to resist militancy targeting "people of all walks of life."[11] The commissioners planned for broad consultations in order to glean ideas from various constituencies. Engaging in these discernments are forms of dialogue that foster trust, rather than simply enhancing police protection in vulnerable sectors. Such approaches resonate with Syed Eshamul Alam's comments in his editorial:

> As a strong nationalist I believed that I along with everyone I have come in contact with embody the ethos of our country; which entails a sense of inclusion, acceptance of diversity and respect for religious freedom. There is a unanimous sense of empathy for all lives lost, civilians and defense forces. Overwhelming support for all those affected is being voiced out everywhere. It begs the question then, why should we as a nation let a group of a few extremists dictate the sentiments of the country?[12]

As stewards of Mystery, the Congregation of Holy Cross remains vigilant about these initiatives and ongoing concerns. In July 2016, at the Notre Dame University of Dhaka, Holy Cross priests, brothers, and sisters, along with lay faculty, staff, and students representing all religions, organized a teach-in and public demonstration in order to highlight the current social and political conditions of Bangladesh. As a symbolic gesture, they peacefully formed a human chain across the campus and into the street to protest the religious fanaticism occurring in the country at present.[13] This gesture reminded them and their constituencies that the defeat of terrorism requires the unification of all members of the Bangladeshi society, which includes processes that remain collaborative in all phases of social justice action, that is, analysis, planning, action, and evaluation.

The story of Holy Cross in Bangladesh illustrates ways in which interreligious friendships continue to foster greater faith and social justice commitments. This history illustrates the importance of sacred conversations and a spirituality of dialogue in recognizing that God's Spirit is at work well ahead of our own plans. This is the source of hope, animating life and ministry as we witness to God's desire for "the transformation of human hearts and relationships."[14]

ACADEMIC CENTERS AND THEOLOGICAL SEMINARIES

Responding to the need to promote better relations among religions, seminaries and universities have created a number of programs for interreligious learning. In 2012, the Association of Theological Schools (ATS) revised its standard for multifaith competencies by identifying the best practices to cultivate intellectual and spiritual hospitality. This revision arose from the ATS two-year project to study ways in which theology programs could enhance multifaith engagement by fostering "an intentional emphasis on interfaith learning."[15]

In challenging schools to reconfigure programs and simply add courses, the ATS project focused on intrinsic motivations for interreligious dialogue within the respective traditions and resources for lifelong learning about the religious others. It was a challenge for the schools to think deeply—to be attentive, intelligent, reasonable, and responsible to their own tradition, while cultivating interreligious relationships. The proposal showed how faculty members recognized the need to be especially attentive to the "heart-knowledge," the shaping of the heart as a critical aspect of multifaith competency.[16]

As noted in part 2, theology programs can avail themselves of the same resources. For example, ATS documented evidence of the success of this approach in its final study showing that theological schools identified competencies from within faith traditions by being both guests of and hosts for other religions.[17] Moreover, the goal for effective interreligious pedagogy can be met by a spirituality of dialogue, contributing to authentic engagement with religions and cultures and creating programs that support a lifelong commitment to sacred conversations.

The Indonesian Immersion: Islam and Christianity course of the Jesuit School of Theology of Santa Clara University (JST) provides another example. Central to this program is a concept of immersion as journeying to Muslim communities and back again to the Catholic "home" tradition. The immersion program succeeded in large part due to the students' spiritual reflections based on the Jesuit practices of spiritual discernment. In the application process, students considered their reasons for taking the course. This discernment pattern continued throughout the course as students and faculty engaged in dialogue with Indonesian Christians and Muslims here in the United States and studied the teachings of Islam and the social history of Indonesia. At the conclusion of these dialogues or study sessions, students and teachers stepped back to "listen to ways" the experiences offered new ideas or challenged them. This process, integral to Jesuit spirituality, reflects the dimensions of sacred conversations.

The deep learning also served as a preparation for a spiritual retreat based on Islamic and Christian mysticism.[18] In the past, retreat evaluations have indicated how well this experience resonates with the students' many contemplative moments throughout the immersion program. Silent reflection helped them to recognize God's Spirit present to them on retreat and throughout the exchanges in the United States and Indonesia. And later, after the student participants returned from Indonesia, they were asked to identify in which ways their experience contributed to theological study and spiritual formation. These evaluations show how the students came to know Indonesian Christians and Muslims as friends who reveal the presence of God. Robert McChesney, SJ, Director of the Jesuit Immersion programs, observes,

When students clamor in their online evaluations for more opportunities for direct encounter with local communities, perhaps this is because such encounters are, in some way to be determined, "intrinsically mystical or sacred." Students sense that they have in some fashion met the sacred in encounter with the Religious Other, which may well explain their enhanced motivation to cultivate such encounters as a lifelong virtue. This component of our model reflects the pedagogical goal of exposing the students to first-hand experience of the sacramentality of the Religious Other.[19]

Sacred conversations enhance interreligious learning as they nurture a spirituality of dialogue capable of integrating interdisciplinary and interreligious study. The Graduate Theological Union (GTU), Berkeley, California, has created a new doctoral program in which students in any given concentration learn how to "read" across religious traditions and disciplines.[20] The reconfigured departments of *Sacred Text and Their Interpretation*, *Historical and Cultural Studies*, *Theology and Ethics*, and *Religion and Practice* represent faculty, students, and community partners' merging research and interests. Sacred conversations are critical to the success of this new program if they foster interreligious learning through the conversion process outlined in part 2. In multifaith settings such as this theological union, comparative studies too often gloss over the faith claims of traditions—study is "about" religions or their spiritualities, not "with" these religions. The latter should include two dimensions: (1) engaging the *whole* of a tradition, including normative claims of a tradition; and (2) fostering partnerships with faith communities. The methodology employed, however, underlines the goal of finding genuine common ground to facilitate religions contributing to theological imaginaries responsive to a culturally and religiously diverse world.[21] Hatem Bazian, cofounder and professor of Zaytuna College, raises concerns about the lack of engagement with metaphysical theory in perceptions about Islam. His discussion about "spiritual materiality" has implications for theological study.

> The word "spiritual"—frequently used in increasingly non-descriptive and narrowly understood ways in the modern and post-colonial period—is a term that postulates a new relationship between the human and God that is no longer regulated by existing "tradition" or normative religious discourses....
>
> The idea of spiritual materiality [is] a concept that I use to show the production of modes of spiritual engagement in the colonial and post-colonial periods that are rooted in elevating the material while totally subverting the centrality of the metaphysical.[22]

Bazian's conclusion highlights the need for systematic study to promote genuine engagement with religions when he says, "Islam's journey in the physical world must begin and end in the metaphysical with everything understood, connected and rooted in it."[23] Sacred conversations seek to explore the depths of faith traditions, and the metaphysical claims of a tradition support these exchanges. Recall the suggestion that Aquinas's and al-Ghazali's virtue theories serve as important resources for sacred conversations, especially in their teachings about perfect happiness with God in this life and the next (*beatitudo* or *as-Sa'ada al-Haqiqiya*), and the ways this goal informs their theological anthropologies.

Regarding the second challenge, that of connecting with faith communities, the GTU has developed a creative approach to fostering this dimension of interreligious learning. For example, in the year 2000, when the GTU schools sought ways to enhance Islamic studies in their programs, the administration had at least two options open to them: (1) seeking donated funds for an Islamic Studies chair, or (2) surveying local Muslim communities for insights and support related to the creation of an Islamic Center. The latter emerged prominent from the quality of dialogues and consultations that took place between the GTU and Bay Area communities. Friendships led to frank and informative encounters that contributed to the creation of the Center for Islamic Studies in 2007 and to the selection of its director, Munir Jiwa. Remaining steadfast in these relationships has supported the continued growth of Islamic studies at the GTU and the ongoing success of the Center for Islamic Studies. Learning across faith communities and the academy stands to transform the next generation of scholars, leaders, and the faith communities represented in the Union.

Thus sacred conversations contribute to theological education and pastoral ministry formation. In formal and informal ways, they facilitate the "passing over" from one's truth to another's truth, the *whole* of it, and back to one's own. As Michael Barnes avers,

> At one point it becomes possible to speak of "we." While remaining members of very different religious traditions, we—interreligious learners— witness not just to particular truths and values sedimented in our funds of ancient wisdom but— more profoundly—to the action of Holy Mystery,

however it be understood, which has made the life of faith possible.[24]

SOCIAL NETWORKING

Historically challenging religious encounters confront us on a daily basis, often casting negative pictures of religion in general or of one particular religion. As indicated above, Christians and Muslims now work cooperatively to reverse troubling trends by promoting interreligious dialogue and study in projects such as A Common Word initiative. I suggest that sacred conversations enhance and expand such commitments.

In a recent essay, Samuel Rizk noted that initiatives need to shift from a "dialogue-as-usual" mentality. The shift requires supportive networks capable of "reducing prejudice and interfaith peace" by bridging concerns through a consistent cross-fertilization of theories and practice.[25]

Rizk's recommendation coincides with Pope Francis's proposal for dialogue in the encyclical *Laudato si* (LS), Care for Our Common Home,[26] a call for all people to dialogue with each other for purposes of creating common ground and stressing the need for personal conversion:

Many things have to change course, but it is we human beings above all who need to change. We lack an awareness of our common origin, of our mutual belonging, and of a future to be shared with everyone. This basic awareness would enable the development of new convictions, attitudes and forms of life. A great cultural, spiritual and educational challenge stands before us, and it will demand that we set out on the long path of renewal. (LS 202)

Francis proposes dialogues as means to promote creativity, honesty, and transparency in the decision-making process. These deliberations, he hopes, will contribute to an "integral ecology," connecting environmental, economic, and spiritual dimensions and resources to offer a holistic personal and communal response to the ecological crisis. In many ways, it represents his "peace document" calling for an active solidarity characterized by the spirituality of dialogue, creating networks that discover new insights (contemplative), lead to deeper understanding of our interconnectedness in God (creative), and challenge us to imagine and contribute to the future that God desires (evolutionary). Catholic, ecumenical, and interreligious partners have reacted positively to the Pope's summons. Recently, the Center of Concern, a Catholic social justice educational organization, formed a new platform for dialogue about the environment called *Integral Voices*[27]—global conversations producing new ideas and innovative projects to promote social justice and peace in the current environmental crisis; these also entail personal conversion. In a recent post, Samuel Zan Akologo stated as much:

Laudato Si has shaped and transformed my conviction, attitude, mind-set, and deep consideration of relationships in and between the environmental and social domains and my personal utilization of both public and private goods. My teenage daughter read *Laudato Si* with ease when I persuaded her to do so and we have since had useful discussions on her perspectives. I am looking forward to her return home from high school on holidays so that I can learn from her about application of *Laudato Si* in a public boarding school environment.[28]

The Center of Concern's new program joins interreligious efforts such as those of Rev. Canon Sally Grover Bingham, who has spent fifteen years building a network as a response to global warming.[29] Evident in this work is the capacity for these conversations to address the spiritual dimensions of this crisis. Through incorporating scientific, practical, and worship resources of various religions, the campaign emphasizes the need for a change in attitudes and habits, looking at the crisis as an opportunity for personal, social, and environmental transformation.

Interreligious dialogical networks give new impetus to human rights programs as well. UNESCO recently created guidelines for developing intercultural competencies and global-intercultural citizenship programs focused on promoting dialogues capable of stimulating "intellectual and moral solidarity."[30] The guidelines state that "social actors need to be able to produce meaningful speech and behaviors and to do so in ways that will be understood as relevant in context by other participants in an interaction."[31] Furthermore, UNESCO identifies a number of specific competencies, including liquidity (flexibility in managing interactions); creativity (drawing from wellsprings of culture, "opening up new forms of dialogue"); and conviviality (changing perception of "the nature of social relationships").[32] These recommendations align well with the integral frame theory mentioned earlier. Effective responses to complex realities, such as addressing human rights concerns in various contexts, require skill sets able to perceive various dimensions of these realities.

All of UNESCO's competencies point to two key factors central to sacred conversations: (1) that persons are transformed by them, referencing the southern African Xhosa proverb, "A person is only a person through other persons" (*ubuntu ngumuntu ngabantu*); and (2) that this transformation is ongoing because relationships change across situations (*Uchi-soto*—the Japanese concept).[33] For this reason, UNESCO has envisioned intercultural competence in its broadest sense as a tree that is rooted in cultures and flourishes through engaging cultural diversity, human rights, and intercultural dialogue.[34] The goals articulated by UNESCO's guidelines correspond to those sought by dialogue participants while engaging in sacred conversations.

Thus the academy, religions, and social justice groups have much in common concerning these pursuits. They find ways to harness resources and foster greater cooperation among them. To this end, Eboo Patel's Interfaith Youth Core offers critical first steps for embracing this transformation.[35] This movement builds bridges of cooperation among students from various religious traditions who share a common life on college campuses. In speaking about the religious pluralism supported by this movement, members of the Core promise "respect for people's diverse religious and non-religious identities" as they seek ways to mutually inspire one another.

Patel speaks of a "science of interfaith cooperation" that "creates positive, meaningful relationships across differences, and fostering appreciative knowledge of other traditions, [and whereby] attitudes improve, knowledge increases, and more relationships occur."[36]

CONCLUSION

The foregoing examples illustrate ways in which a spirituality of dialogue nurtured by sacred conversations animate interreligious learning, foster friendships, and promote collaboration for social-environmental justice. Reversing the troubling trend of negative views about Islam requires new models for dialogue. On the tenth anniversary of the September 11, 2001, terrorist attacks, Reverend William Ledens, CSSP, and I organized a gathering with the Graduate Theological Union, Newman Center of the University of California, and Zaytuna College, the first accredited Muslim liberal arts college in USA, titled, "Conversations We Never Had."[37]

The program focused on how dialogues and educational programs immediately following these attacks were energetic and vast, yet they failed to address deep concerns and did not consider plans for ongoing engagement. Sacred conversations present powerful opportunities to reignite this initial zeal and enhance the much-needed dialogues because they connect participants with the interior movements of the Spirit. Sacred conversations release a spiritual power, that is, "the love and compassion" that Teilhard de Chardin claims is the future of all the earth.[38] With a commitment to dialogue and learning, people of all faiths realize how "the Spirit of God has filled the universe with possibilities and therefore, from the very heart of things, something new can always emerge" (LS 80). Sr. Madeleva Wolff, CSC, speaks of this in her evocative 1944 convocation address for Saint Mary's College, Notre Dame, Indiana: "Tomorrow, and tomorrow, and tomorrow lie before you and your undiscovered worlds.…You are co-creators of worlds of the mind, bringing tidings of truth into a future yet unguessed by you."[39]

The following poem by Sr. Eva Mary Hooker, CSC, echoes this hope:

> *(I called and called*
> *and the Spirit of Wisdom came to me)—*

just so, fierce knowing prints
Wisdom upon us,

the center of our common gravity,
and pulls us to her

and holds us fast in cords, tenderly, heart-root
of grace:

> *(I called and called*
> *and the Spirit of Wisdom came to me)—*

Perhaps this is a new genesis, a paradigm shift such as Brian P. Hall described. This "genesis effect" occurs when the global community moves from understanding the world as a place to fear, a problem to be solved, or even a project to complete, to recognizing it as a mystery to embrace.[40] Sacred conversations seek to embrace this mystery. And it will take the communication with and cooperation of all cultures and religions—indeed of all those who think differently—for humankind to hold in esteem the unconfused, complex, and enthused connection that exists between living beings and the Spirit of Wisdom who guides us all.

RESPONSE TO THE MADELEVA
LECTURE DELIVERED BY
SISTER MARIANNE FARINA, 2016

First of all, I am delighted to have been invited to respond to the Madeleva lecture given by Marianne Farina, CSC, who over the years has become a close, dear friend and colleague. We met almost immediately after I came to Notre Dame in 1996—it is hard to believe that was 20 years ago—where I taught for thirteen years before leaving for Indiana University. Our paths continued to cross during those thirteen years, especially at the Center for Spirituality at Saint Mary's. At Marianne's invitation, I joined the Voices of Vision seminar for a couple of years. I was also privileged to attend a number of Madeleva lectures at Saint Mary's of which I have such fond memories. It is good to be reminded from time to time that theology is not the exclusive prerogative of men and that highly intelligent women of faith are making important differences in the quality and tenor of life everywhere, even if it mostly happens under the radar. Happily, our paths have continued to cross through the years even after my departure from South Bend, especially at various symposia focused on interfaith dialogue.

Marianne's impassioned and moving essay expresses her own personal commitment to the sacred task of opening avenues of conversation and service between different faith communities, particularly between Christians and Muslims, in the name of the one God we love and serve. As she herself states, her own dedication to interfaith dialogue is undergirded by the statement contained in clause no. 3 in the CSC constitution: "Everything we are and do must communicate our commitment to God's desire for the transformation of human hearts and human relationships."

Here I am reminded of the Qur'an's emphasis on the transformation of human hearts as a prelude to a meaningful relationship with God and with one's fellow human beings. In one of its best-known and much-cited verses, the Qur'an (in chap. 13, v. 11) states, "Indeed, God does not change people's circumstances unless they change what is in themselves." According to this verse, change is to be effected first internally in the individual before any meaningful external change can take root. The most important site for bringing about genuine individual change followed by social change is thus clearly the human heart. Transformation of the human heart occurs by making it receptive to God's will and becoming filled with God-consciousness. In Arabic, this God-consciousness is termed *taqwa*, as Marianne mentions, referring to the inner piety that transforms our relationship not only with the Almighty but also with our neighbors and all those we meet in the course of our lives. Both our faith traditions emphasize the importance of this principle of reconciliation with our Creator and his created beings, and both emphasize the necessity of this inner transformation that we must undergo for assuming a life of service to others.

When I taught courses on Islam at Notre Dame, I would explain the principle of *taqwa* to my primarily Catholic students as being equivalent in the Christian milieu to being filled with the Holy Spirit, and at once they would understand it. Being filled with *taqwa* or the Holy Spirit in each tradition is similarly understood to be fundamentally transformative of the human being so that even mundane actions are endowed with greater meaning and depth.

Marianne importantly emphasizes that we "communicate" God's desire for this transformation in us by building up a society of justice and love. Too often, pious intent remains at the level of words only and righteousness consists of *not* doing certain things rather than proactively doing things. A more positive, service-oriented notion of piety requires us to work toward a society that is full of compassion and justice, particularly toward its disadvantaged members, and to cultivate an attitude of openness to the so-called other—particularly those who practice a religion different from ours, those who speak a different language, and those who have different cultural practices. From the Qur'an (49:13) we derive the concept of *ta'aruf*—getting to know one another and celebrating one another's differences even as we seek commonly shared values. In the Christian tradition, this would be equivalent to hospitality, which similarly emphasizes "an openness to difference" that leads to "more profound self-knowledge."

It is fitting that Marianne should end her inspirational talk by emphasizing hope to which God calls us to bear witness. Both Christianity and Islam are founded on hope. The Qur'an and the Bible assure us that we must never despair of God's love and solicitude for us and never lose faith in the ultimate goodness of human beings. The well-known Islamic concept of *fitra* underscores how humans are wired to be good and to carry out acts of goodness. When we fail to do so, we fail ourselves and others as human beings. We realize our fullest potential as human beings when we live up to this mandate to seek the best in ourselves and in others through love of God and sincere servitude to him. Marianne mentions the "Common Word" statement that emphasizes the bedrock tenet of both Islam and Christianity—the love of God and neighbor.

As many of you may already know, the "Common Word" statement invokes Qur'an 3:64, a verse that in recent times has received much attention in interfaith circles. This verse states,

> Say, "O People of the Book, let us come to a common word (*kalima sawa'*) between us and you that we will worship only the one God and not ascribe any partner to Him nor should any of us take others as lords besides the one God." If they should turn their backs, say, "Bear witness that we submit to God" (*muslimun*).

Many exegetes commenting on Qur'an 3:64 are in agreement that *kalima sawa'* is primarily a reference to "a word of justice," a gloss that in itself is open to further interpretation. "Justice" is thus variously interpreted as "sincerity" by one early exegete named Muqatil b. Sulayman (d. 767), as "upright" and an assertion of the oneness of God by the celebrated exegetes al-Tabari

(d. 923) and al-Zamakhshari (d. 1144), and as "fair" and "equitable" by the influential Qur'an commentator al-Razi (d. 1210).

It is highly significant that in 2007, the Qur'anic phrase *kalima sawa'* was invoked by 138 Muslim scholars and clerics in a statement addressed to Christian religious leaders of various denominations that became known as "A Common Word" statement. With interpretive creativity, the Muslim signatories to the "Common Word" statement may be regarded as having distilled these various significations of justice into the pithy commandment "Love God and your neighbor." Such interpretive discernment in the context of dialogue was clearly born of deep reflection on the whys and wherefores of interfaith encounters and existential necessity. In our fractious and fragile post–September 11 world, a common word must of necessity be a word that at the very least unites and creates common ground on the basis of shared beliefs and values.

The reaction from many Christian leaders has been positive, proving that the premise of the "Common Word" statement clearly struck a chord among people of goodwill. After the issuance of the statement, three high-level meetings between Christian and Muslim scholars and religious leaders occurred between 2007 and 2008. The first was a well-publicized conference at the Yale Divinity School at which Muslim and Christian theologians took up the two main themes of the "Common Word." Subsequently, a letter signed by three hundred prominent Protestant theologians and scholars endorsing the Common Word initiative was published in the *New York Times*. The second meeting was hosted by Cambridge University in

England in October and ended with a meeting with the then Archbishop of Canterbury, Dr. Rowan Williams, at Lambeth Palace in London. Prior to the October meeting, the archbishop wrote a profound and moving response to the "Common Word" statement, underscoring "what could be the centre of a sense of shared calling and shared responsibility" with the statement's focus on love of God and neighbor. The third meeting took place at the Vatican in Rome on November 4–6, 2008, as the first seminar of the Catholic-Muslim Forum in which roughly sixty Muslim and Catholic religious leaders and scholars from various parts of the world participated. Subsequent meetings have taken place at Georgetown University and the Vatican.

The last time Marianne and I met was at a Common Word follow-up conference held in Dublin, Ireland, at Mater Dei University. The proceedings of this conference will soon be published by Cambridge University Press, and therefore some of the wonderful papers presented there will soon be available to a broader readership. The palpable goodwill and genuine meeting of minds between Christians and Muslims that we encountered there was not uncommon at all. Such cultivation of goodwill and seeking common purpose have been an express objective of the "Common Word" declaration, and much good continues to come out of the activities that have been organized to attempt to fulfill its lofty goals.

In her most perceptive talk today, Marianne shows us that we can find this common ground through dialogue, what she calls "sacred conversations." I loved Marianne's emphasis on these "sacred conversations," the practice of which, she affirms, undergirds the apostolic mission of the Sisters of the Holy Cross, whom she so ably represents and from whose ranks came Sr. Madeleva, whose name we commemorate today. Dialogue that is truly fruitful and truly sacred must, however, be conducted in the proper spirit and with the respect it deserves. Marianne picks humility and hospitality as the two essential virtues we must bring to the conversation table, for they are, she says, "the cornerstones of a spirituality of dialogue." Such a perspective resonates strongly within the Islamic milieu as well. Small wonder then that Thomas Aquinas and al-Ghazali—two intellectual giants in the premodern world, Christian and Muslim respectively—both acknowledge the importance of these virtues for proper knowledge of the self and its relationship to God. Today we would add that these virtues are essential for conducting sacred conversations with one another that allow us to celebrate our interconnectedness and to remind us that we have a common responsibility to uphold and promote what is good and prevent what is wrong as part of our common stewardship on earth.

Sacred conversations help to keep this compact among ourselves alive and relevant. And most importantly of all, these sacred conversations help us to push back against profane conversations that seek to divide and foment hatred, of which unfortunately there has been way too much lately.

Asma Afsaruddin
Professor of Islamic Studies
Indiana University, Bloomington

POEMS BY
EVA MARY HOOKER, CSC

Analogy of the Bee and the Pulley

Just as the bee pulls the line,
hind legs low, flying

in free air, its back curved to lift
the plank of missing words:

> *(I called and called*
> *and the Spirit of Wisdom came to me)*—

just so, fierce knowing prints
Wisdom upon us,

the center of our common gravity,
and pulls us to her

and holds us fast in cords, tenderly, heart-root
of grace:

> *(I called and called*
> *and the Spirit of Wisdom came to me)*—

just so the pulley, her formal courtesy and practical radiance,
is made to draw

us up to the mirror
of Wisdom—

(*reflection of eternal light*)—She,

whom we are able to take into our hands.

Mirror of moons: a *goostly beholding*

of grace

taught from within the mystery—heart-root

veiled.

Serenitas

In shadow of moon we walk the sycamores—

~

Women wrap their kneading bowls in cloaks
   of wool flee homeland weep brown tears sew wedding
      jewels into the hems of their garments pick spikelets
         of lavender
         work olive oil into their hair against the heat
            preserve the sound of desert swales blowing
               walk out past privacy of stone—

~

Hold fast the mirror, she says.

Test your stirrings she says thoroughly test your stirrings
   take care by the scruff of its weary neck
let it wrinkle your face like hers give you direct gaze into
   within so that *soul melts into air anima*
into aura—and—

Serenitas.

She says, hold on to word. Who knows my dwelling
   place?

Who knows the reckoning of
my moons?

(Grace is the Within of God)—[1]

Come and tell what its form may be:

Come and tell—

Come out, God in.
Come out, God in.

Come out, God in.
Come out, God in.

~

She carries remnants, day-break and ripe fig. The smell of
lemon, the baby's harness crossed over her shoulder, sun
that hurts her eyes. She walks in bare feet towards the sea
and the purple-red of sun down. Passes the girls' school,
closed after the violent season. Waits for dark in her blue
dress. She crosses into miles of nothing. Spectral land from
which the tide of sand goes out in quiet laps of red-brown.
She walks on, kneels at the edge of the water, kisses the
shore, place where his head was taken from his body. She
walks into the tide. Then out, then in. Then out, then in.
Out and on into the shimmering down-lit light. Her baby
cries. A gentle shush and she walks on—

~

In shadow of moon: we walk the sycamores—
In shadow of moon we walk
the sycamores—

1. The line in italics is from "Granum Sinapsis," translated by Bernard
McGinn.

NOTES

INTRODUCTION

1. Examples include Georgetown University's Prince Alwaleed bin Talal Center for Muslim-Christian Understanding (https://acmcu.georgetown.edu), USCCB Office for Ecumenical and Interreligious Affairs (http://www.usccb.org/beliefs-and-teachings/ecumenical-and-interreligious/index.cfm), The Building Bridges Seminars of the Anglican Church (https://berkleycenter.georgetown.edu/projects/the-building-bridges-seminar), Salam Peace and Justice Institute (http://salaminstitute.org/new/), and A Common Word initiative (http://www.acommonword.com/).

2. Organizations like the Islamic Networks Group and the Compassionate Listening Project offer programs for developing dialogue and listening skills. See http://www.ing.org and http://www.compassionatelistening.org.

3. John Borelli, ed., *A Common Word and the Future of Muslim-Christian Relations*, ACMCU Occasional Papers, June 2009, https://acmcu.georgetown.edu/research/papers.

4. Michael O'Loughlin, "Report Finds U.S. Catholics Have Much to Learn about Islam," *America Magazine*, September 12, 2016, http://www.americamagazine.org/content/dispatches/report-finds-us-catholics-much-learn-about-islam?utm_source=Full+List+with+Groups&utm

_campaign=6b850f9ab2-Web_Content_9_14_169_14
_2016&utm_medium=email&utm_term=0_0fe8ed70be
-6b850f9ab2-57375113.

5. John Dunne, *The Way of All the Earth* (New York: Macmillan, 1972), 12.

PART I

1. Report of News Agency interviewing John XXIII about the need for a council. S.v. "John XXIII," in http://newworldencyclopedia.org (accessed October 8, 2016).

2. John Borelli, "A New Era and a New Model for Christian-Muslim Dialogue," in *Nostra Aetate: Celebrating 50 Years of the Catholic Church's dialogue with Jews and Muslims*, ed. Pim Valkenberg and Anthony Cirelli (Washington, DC: Catholic University Press, 2016), 98–99.

3. John Courtney Murray, *We Hold These Truths: Catholic Reflections on the American Proposition* (London: Sheed & Ward, 2005), 31. This is a new edition of Murray's 1960 collection of essays with a new introduction by Peter Augustine Lawler.

4. *Congregation of the Sisters of the Holy Cross, Constitutions and Statutes* (Notre Dame, IN: Sisters of the Holy Cross, 1982), 4–5.

5. Ibid., 4.

6. Ibid.

7. Ibid., 1.

8. Basil Moreau, "Circular Letter #14," in *Circular Letters of Basil Moreau* (Notre Dame, IN: Ave Maria Press, 1944), 38–45.

9. World Parliament of Religions Statement, https://berkleycenter.georgetown.edu/publications/declaration-toward-a-global-ethic.

10. Timothy Wright, *No Peace without Prayer: Encouraging Muslims and Christians to Pray Together* (Collegeville, MN: Liturgical Press, 2013), 32.

11. Lee Yearly, *Mencius and Aquinas: Theories of Virtue and Conceptions of Courage* (Albany, NY: SUNY Press, 1990), 175–82, 169–75.

12. Bl. Basil Moreau, *Circular Letter* #36, in *Circular Letters*. "We can state the kind of teaching we hope to give….Even though we base our philosophy on faith, no one need fear that we will confine our teaching within narrow and unscientific boundaries. We will accept the discoveries of science without prejudice, and in a manner adapted to the needs of our times. We do not want our students to be ignorant of anything they should know….We will always place education side by side with instruction; the mind will not be cultivated at the expense of the heart."

13. Bl. Basil Anthony M. Moreau, *Christian Education*, 5, first published in 1856, now available at http://www.holycrossinstitute.org/sites/default/files/u11/christian_education.pdf. He says, "To teach with success, teachers must know good methods, be skillful in applying them…all these are acquired and perfected through study…as much as they can."

PART II

1. Pontifical Council for Interreligious Dialogue, *Guidelines for Dialogue between Christians and Muslims*, Interreligious Documents 1 (Mahwah, NJ: Paulist Press, 1981), 1.

2. This passage from the Qur'an cited in "A Common Word" can be found at http://www.acommonword.com/the-acw-document/ (accessed October 20, 2016).

3. John Borelli, "A New Era and a New Model for Christian-Muslim Dialogue," in *A Common Word and the Future of Muslim-Christian Relations*, ACMCU Occasional Papers, June 2009, 106, https://acmcu.georgetown.edu/research/papers. See also http://www.usccb.org/beliefs-and-teachings/ecumenical-and-interreligious/interreligious/islam/ (accessed October 14, 2016).

4. Borelli, "A New Era," 107.

5. John Andrew Morrow, *The Covenants of the Prophet Muhammad with the Christians of the World* (San Bernardino, CA: Sophia Perennis, 2014), xv.

6. David Thomas, ed., *Christian-Muslim Relations: A Bibliographic History*, 8 vols. (London: Brill, 2009–16).

7. Muhammad Shafiq and Mohammed Abu-Nimer, *Interfaith Dialogue: A Guide for Muslims* (Herndon, VA: International Institute of Islamic Thought, 2007), 43–46.

8. Ibid., 64.

9. Ibid., 65.

10. "A Common Word" (Jordan: The Royal Aal al-Bayt Institute for Islamic Thought, 2007), http://www.acommonword.com/the-acw-document/ (emphasis mine).

11. Final Declaration of the "First Seminar of the Catholic-Muslim Forum," Rome, November 4–6, 2008, 3–4. Full text available at http://www.asianews.it/index.php?l=en&art=13687.

12. Bernard Lonergan, *Method in Theology* (Toronto: University of Toronto Press, 1971), 14–15.

13. Ibid., 35.

14. Ibid., 57.

15. Ibid., 238–44.

16. Stephen Bevans and Robert Schroeder, *Prophetic Dialogue: Reflection on Christian Mission Today* (Maryknoll, NY: Orbis Books, 2011), 21.

17. Lonergan, *Method in Theology*, 238.

18. James Fowler, *Stages of Faith, Psychology of Human Development and the Quest for Meaning* (New York: Harper-Collins, 1995), 72–75, 78–79, 244.

19. Ibid., 30.

20. Lonergan, *Method in Theology*, 240.

21. JustFaith Ministries, http://justfaith.org/about-us/history-mission/.

22. Lonergan, *Method in Theology*, 240–41.

23. Thomas Aquinas, *Summa Theologiae*, II, II, q. 27, art 1, ad 2.

24. Lonergan, *Method in Theology*, 241.

25. C. G. Jung, *Psychology and Religion* (New York: Pantheon, 1958), 105.

26. John Dunne, *The Way of All the Earth*, 221 (see intro., n. 5).

27. Thomas Aquinas: "We ought to consider human beings more worthy than other creatures and not in any way diminish human dignity either through sin or an inordinate desire for material things....Rather we ought to prize ourselves in the way God made us." *The Sermon Conferences of Saint Thomas Aquinas on the Apostles' Creed*, ed. N. Ayo (Notre Dame, IN: University of Notre Dame Press, 1988), 43.

Al-Ghazali: "[Humans were] not created in jest or at random, but are marvelously made for some great end. Although he is not from everlasting, yet he will live forever; and though his body is mean and earthly, yet his spirit will be made lofty and divine." *Al-Ghazali on Disciplining the Soul, Kitab Riyadat al-nafs and Breaking the*

Two Desires, Kitab Kasr al-shahwatayn. Books XXII and XXIII of the Revival of the Religious Sciences, Ihya ulum al-din, trans. T. J. Winter (Cambridge: Islamic Texts Society, 1997), 14; and *Alchemy of Happiness (Kimia-ya sa adat)*, trans. Claude Field (Armonk, NY: M. E. Sharpe, 1991), 10.

28. Thomas Aquinas, *Summa Theologica*, First Complete American Edition in Three Volumes, trans. Fathers of the English Dominican Province (New York: Benziger, 1947). All references are from this edition.

29. Servais Pinckaers, *Morality: The Catholic View*, trans. Mary Thomas Noble, OP (Washington, DC: Catholic University Press, 1995), 87.

30. "The spiritual increase of charity may be considered in respect of a certain likeness to the growth of the human body. For although this latter growth may be divided into many parts, yet it has certain fixed divisions according to those particular actions or pursuits to which man is brought by this same growth. Thus we speak of a man being an infant until he has the use of reason, after which we distinguish another state of man wherein he begins to speak and use reason, while there is a third state, that of puberty, when he begins to acquire the power of generation and so on until he arrives at perfection" (ST II-II 24.9).

31. Pinckaers, *Morality*, 375.

32. Ibid., 367. Pinckaers says, "Our freedom reaches maturity precisely with our capacity to balance the two-fold dimension of personality and openness to others, interiority and outreach, living 'for self' and 'for others.' We should note here that only the concept of freedom for excellence, based on a natural sense of the true and the

good, enables us to be aware of this association, so vital for moral theory" (ibid.).

33. Sachiko Murata and William C. Chittick, *The Vision of Islam* (St. Paul, MN: Paragon Press, 1994), 288.

Islam or the Shariah is concerned with differentiating right activity from wrong activity and explaining how to do things correctly....

Iman adds a dimension of understanding. It allows people to see that the meaning of activity transcends the domain of everyday life and reaches back into the divine reality. It lets them understand that everything in the universe is governed by *tawhid*, yet human freedom of choice can upset the balance....

Ihsan adds to *islam* and *iman* a focus on intentionality. It directs human beings to reorient their desiring and choosing on the basis of an awareness of God's presence in all things. (288)

34. Mohamed Sherif, *Al-Ghazali's Theory of Virtue* (Albany, NY: NY State University Press, 1975), 31.

35. Al-Ghazali's works on the moral and spiritual life have been translated into English, especially his major works *Ihya ulum al din (Revival of Religious Sciences)* and *Kimiya-al sa'adat (Alchemy of Happiness)*. Reference to these translations, along with original Arabic can be located at http://www.ghazali.org.

36. Sherif, *Al-Ghazali's Theory of Virtue*, 24, 77, 105.

37. Ghazali's teaching emphasizes the need for transforming the heart. Muslims believe that the heart is the human dwelling place of the good that originates in God. In *Ihya* he writes, "The heart is such that if man knows

it, he indeed knows himself, he indeed knows his Lord. It is also the heart which, if a man does not know it, he indeed knows not himself: and if he knows not himself, he indeed knows not his lord—and one who knows not his heart, is even more ignorant of other things." Al-Ghazali, *Kitab Sharh Aja'ib al-Qalb (The Book of the Marvels of the Heart)*, trans. R. J. McCarthy in *Deliverance from Error* (Louisville, KY: Fons Vitae, 2000), 310.

38. Al-Ghazali, *Alchemy of Happiness*, 3–4.

39. Mara Brecht, *Virtues in Dialogue: Belief, Religious Diversity and Women's Interreligious Dialogue* (Eugene, OR: Pickwick Publications, 2014), 131.

40. Ibid., 149, 152.

41. Ibid., 144.

42. Frank Clooney, *Comparative Theology: Deep Learning across Religious Borders* (Malden, MA: Wiley-Blackwell, 2010), 68.

43. Ibid., 13.

44. Ibid., 61.

45. Ibid., 64.

46. See https://berkleycenter.georgetown.edu/projects/the-building-bridges-seminar (accessed May 2, 2016). The whole series is documented in fourteen books. The books are a great resource for dialogues and academic courses on dialogue.

47. His Royal Highness Prince El Hasan bin Talal of Jordan, Opening Address, *The Road Ahead: A Christian-Muslim Dialogue*, ed. Michael Ipgrave (London: Church House Publishing, 2002), xi.

48. Rowan Williams, *Death, Resurrection and Human Destiny: Christian-Muslim Perspectives*, ed. David Marshall and Lucinda Mosher (Washington, DC: Georgetown University Press, 2014), xxii.

49. Catherine Cornille, *The Impossibility of Interreligious Dialogue* (New York: Herder & Herder, 2008), 2.

50. Ibid., 4–6.

51. Ibid., 3.

52. Amos Yong addresses the importance of hospitality in learning how to be hosts and guests in multifaith contexts. See his *Hospitality and the Other: Pentecost, Christian Practices, and the Neighbor* (Maryknoll, NY: Orbis Books, 2008), 153–56.

53. James L. Fredericks, "Interreligious Friendship: A New Theological Virtue," *Journal of Ecumenical Studies* 35, no. 2 (Spring 1998): 159–60.

54. Ibid.

55. Lonergan, *Method in Theology*, 241.

56. Bede Griffiths, *The Marriage of East and West: A Sequel to the Golden String* (Springfield, IL: Templegate Publishers, 1982), 151.

57. Bede Griffiths, *The Cosmic Revelation* (Springfield, IL: Templegate, 1983), 30.

58. A discussion of Merton's relationship with Buddhism and a bibliography of his books about Buddhism is located at http://www.thomasmertonsociety.org/altany2.htm (accessed March 2, 2017).

59. Gray Henry and Rob Baker, *Merton and Sufism: The Untold Story: A Complete Compendium* (Louisville, KY: Fons Vitae, 1999).

60. Barbara Marx Hubbard, "Standing at the Crossroads: It is in Our Hands," seminar by Lynn M. Levo, Sisters of the Holy Cross, April 8, 2013.

61. Claire Zammit and Katherine Woodward Thomas, "Standing at the Crossroads."

62. Ilia Delio, ed., "Evolution and the Rise of the Secular God," in *From Teilhard to Omega* (Maryknoll, NY: Orbis Books, 2014), 49–50, 196.

63. Martin Nowak, *SuperCooperators: Altruism, Evolution, and Why We Need Each Other to Succeed* (New York: Free Press, 2011), xvii.

64. Ibid., 274–75.

65. Ibid.

66. Ibid., 276.

67. Ibid.

68. Ibid., 277.

69. Alan Watkins and Ken Wilber, *Wicked and Wise: How to Solve the World's Toughest Problems* (Kent: Urbane Publications, 2015), 53–55.

70. Ibid., 60.

71. Ibid., 68–69, 99–103.

72. David Tracy, "Theology: Comparative Theology," in *Encyclopedia of Religion*, vol. xiv (New York: Macmillan, 1986), 446.

73. Diarmuid O'Murchu, *Poverty, Celibacy, and Obedience: A Radical Option for Life* (New York: Crossroads, 1999), 26. O'Murchu speaks about vowed life, but his analysis and reflection address how people of faith will also find themselves called to Poverty (stewardship), Celibacy (right relationships), and Obedience (mutual relations—empowerment).

PART III

1. Kamruddin Ahman, *A Social History of Bangladesh* (Dhaka: Progoti Publishers, 1967), xxi.

2. Raymond J. Clancy, *The Congregation of Holy Cross in East Bengal, 1853–1953* (Washington, DC: Holy Cross Foreign Mission Seminary, 1952), 1:50.

3. Canon Etienne Catta and Tony Catta, *Basil Anthony Mary Moreau*, trans. Edward L. Heston, CSC (Milwaukee, WI: Bruch Publishing Company, 1955), 1:908.

4. See http://www.newworldencyclopedia.org/entry/Bangladesh_War_of_Independence. The Bangladesh Constitution that emerged put religious freedom central to the new republic. See especially amendment no. 45; http://www.wipo.int/wipolex/en/text.jsp?file_id=191721. Also see the interview with Rev. Richard Timm, CSC, https://berkleycenter.georgetown.edu/interviews/a-discussion-with-father-richard-william-timm-congregation-of-holy-cross.

5. Bl. Basil Moreau, *Circular Letter* #10, in *Circular Letters* (see part 1, n. 8).

6. In Jalchatra, the women's cooperatives were not just forums for creating handicraft jute items and marketing them but also became places where we shared about our lives and learned from one another. We also engaged in an intertextual exercise with Muslims, Christians, and Hindus about protecting the environment. This later project was reported in my article "A Response to Terry Muck," *Interpretation: A Journal of Bible and Theology* (January 2007): 24–27.

7. "Think of us in this way, as servants of Christ and stewards of God's mysteries. Moreover, it is required of stewards that they be found trustworthy" (1 Cor 4:1–2, NRSV).

8. Qur'an 4:128 and 2:233.

9. Masarrat Khan, "Friendship: Cultivating Theological Virtue," in *Interreligious Friendships after* Nostra Aetate, ed. James Fredericks and Tracy Sayuki Tiemeier (New York: Palgrave MacMillan, 2015), 63.

10. Chris Herlinger, "Q & A with Sr. Violet Rodrigues: Educating girls in Muslim Bangladesh," *Global Sisters Report*, January 14, 2016, accessed April 2, 2016, http://globalsistersreport.org/blog/q/ministry/q-sr-violet -rodrigues-educating-girls-muslim-bangladesh-36366.

11. "DC Conference Beings July 26," *The Daily Star*, July 24, 2016, http://www.thedailystar.net/city/dc -conference-begins-july-26-1258609.

12. Syed Eshamul Alam, "Extremists Cannot Dictate the Sentiments of Bangladesh," *The Daily Star*, July 6, 2016, http://epaper.dawn.com/DetailImage.php ?StoryImage=06_07_2016_011_003.

13. "Human Chain Protesting Terrorism at Notre Dame University," *N-TV Online*, Bangladesh News Agency, August 1, 2016, http://m.en.ntvbd.com/education/ 29801/Human-chain-protesting-terrorism-at-Notre -Dame-University.

14. Sisters of the Holy Cross, *Constitution and Statutes*, 3.

15. Stephen R. Graham, "Christian Hospitality and Pastoral Practices in a Multifaith Society: An ATS Project 2010–2012," *Theological Education* 47, no. 1 (2012): 12.

16. Sang-Ehil Han, Paul Louis Metzger, and Terry C. Muck, "Christian Hospitality and Pastoral Perspectives from an Evangelical Perspective," *Theological Education* 47, no. 1 (2012): 23.

17. For example, see Eleazar S. Fernandez, "Christian Hospitality in a World on Many Faiths: Equipping the New Generation of Religious Leaders in a Multifaith

Context," *Theological Education* 47, no. 2 (2013); and Amos Yong, "Guests of Religious Others: Theological Education in the Pluralistic World," *Theological Education* 47, no. 1 (2012).

18. The retreat was directed by Dr. Syafaatun Almirzanah and me and it focused on her work. Syafaatun Almirzanah, *When Mystic Masters Meet: Toward a New Matrix for Christian-Muslim Dialogue* (Clifton, NJ: Blue Dome Press, 2011).

19. Robert McChesney and Marianne Farina, "A Contextual Model for Teaching and Assessing Interreligious Encounters," in American Academy of Religion's Study on *Interreligious Encounters* (forthcoming).

20. See http://gtu.edu/academics/departments-concentrations.

21. Michael Barnes, *Interreligious Learning: Dialogue, Spirituality and the Christian Imagination* (Cambridge, UK: Cambridge University Press, 2012), 23.

22. Hatem Bazian, "The Metaphysical and the Crisis of Spiritual Materiality," October 26, 2016, http://www.hatembazian.com/content/the-metaphysical-and-the-crisis-of-spiritual-materiality/.

23. Ibid.

24. Barnes, *Interreligious Learning*, 264.

25. Samuel Rizk, "Christian-Muslim Relations in the Middle East: Reflections on Dialogue and Post-Dialogue," in *A Common Word and the Future of Muslim-Christian Relations*, ACMCU Occasional Papers, June 2009, 75–77, https://acmcu.georgetown.edu/research/papers.

26. Pope Francis, *Laudato si*, Care for Our Common Home, May 24, 2015, http://w2.vatican.va/content/francesco/en/encyclicals/documents/papa-francesco_20150524_enciclica-laudato-si.html.

27. See https://integral-voices.com/.

28. Ibid.

29. See http://www.interfaithpowerandlight.org/.

30. United Nations Education, Scientific, and Cultural Organization, *Intercultural Competencies: Conceptual and Operational Framework* (Paris: UNESCO, 2013), 4, http://en.unesco.org/cultureofpeace/intercultural-competences-in-peace/human-rights-democracy-and-peace.

31. Ibid., 17.

32. Ibid., 18–20.

33. Ibid., 20–21.

34. Ibid., 23.

35. See https://www.ifyc.org/about.

36. Ibid.

37. See http://calnewman.org/students/stories/ (accessed October 20, 2016).

38. Ilia Delio, "Evolution and the Rise of the Secular God," in *From Teilhard to Omega*, ed. Ilia Delio (Maryknoll, NY: Orbis Books, 2014), 49.

39. Quoted in Frances B. O'Connor, "Bangladesh," in *International Conference on Christianity and Native Cultures* (Notre Dame, IN: Saint Mary's College, 2002).

40. Brian T. Hall, *Value Shift: A Guide to Personal and Organizational Transformation* (Rockport, MA: Twin Lights Publishing, 1994), 46.